# THE WOUNDED STAG

William Johnston, an Irish Jesuit, was formerly Professor of Religious Studies at Sophia University in Tokyo, and Director of the Institute of Oriental Studies in Tokyo. He now teaches prayer and meditation in the Philippines.

He has written extensively on Eastern and Western mysticism, has lectured throughout Europe, Australia and North America, and is actively involved in Christian-Buddhist dialogue. He is the author of *Silent Music, The Inner Eye of Love* and *The Mirror Mind* (all available as Fount Paperbacks), as well as of *The Mysticism of the Cloud of Unknowing, The Still Point,* and *Christian Zen.*

*For*
*Juan Diego*
*and*
*The Woman*
*he loves*

First published in 1984 as *Christian Mysticism Today*
by William Collins Sons & Co Ltd, London
and by Harper & Row Publishers, Inc, New York
Published in Great Britain as *The Wounded Stag*
by Fount Paperbacks, London in 1985

© Copyright William Johnston 1984

Made and printed in Great Britain
by William Collins Sons & Co Ltd, Glasgow

William
Johnston

# THE
# WOUNDED
# STAG

"The Wounded Stag
   Appears
  On the Hill"

ST JOHN OF THE CROSS

Collins
FOUNT PAPERBACKS

# Contents

# 1

# The
# Desert

I

In the year of Our Lord 1981, when Menachem Begin was Prime Minister in Israel and Anwar Sadat was President of Egypt, I had the privilege of spending six months in Jerusalem. I lived at an institute on the outskirts of the holy city with a motley group of scripture scholars, each of whom pursued his or her biblical project with admirable enthusiasm and devotion. My project (and what a project!) was to study the roots of Christian mysticism. Having spent many years comparing Christian mysticism with its Buddhist counterpart, having searched for similarities and explored common ground, I felt that the time had come to investigate the unique dimension of the Christian experience and to look for its distinctive features. In doing this I wanted to go beyond St. John of the Cross and St. Teresa of Avila, beyond Meister Eckhart and *The Cloud of Unknowing*, beyond Augustine and Gregory, to the very origins of that mystical prayer which assumes increasing significance in the lives of contemporary men and women.

I suspected that I would find what I wanted in the desert. After all, was it not in the desert that the people of Israel

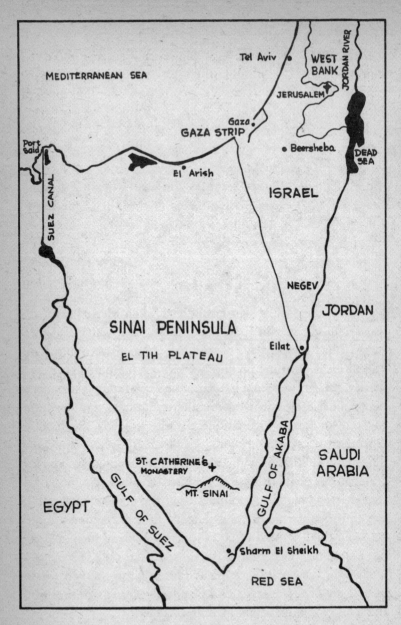

SINAI: The Great and Terrible Wilderness

experienced the steadfast love of Yahweh and entered into covenant with Him? Was it not in the desert that the word came to John the Baptist? Was it not in the wilderness that Jesus prayed and fasted before meeting the devil? And the early Christian monks fled from pagan Rome into the rich silence of the desert where they prayed and fasted and bequeathed to us an invaluable treasury of spiritual maxims and mystical counsel.

So I spent considerable time in the desert—in the Judean desert, in the Negev, in Sinai, and finally in the Egyptian desert south of Alexandria. I came to love the Dead Sea. I was fascinated by Jericho and by that monastery perched high on the cliff called "the mount of temptations." Early in the morning, before any tourist appeared, I stood at Qumran, home of those extraordinary Essenes, relishing the empty stillness which hovered over the wilderness and over the sea. It all reminded me of the rich atmosphere one finds in some Buddhist temples, except that here I sensed that obscure and indefinable sense of presence that one necessarily associates with the monotheistic religions. And it became clear to me that environment creates religious experience. Environment can lead to an altered state of consciousness. Perhaps it creates something like mystical experience. One discovers that the vast and empty desert is not only "out there"; it is also "in here." One enters the inner desert. And perhaps Jesus and John the Baptist did just that.

And Sinai—"that great and terrible wilderness" (Deuteronomy 1:19)! There, too, the immensity and the awesome beauty seemed to create religious experience. I had not expected such variety of scenery; and as I saw the miles and miles of brown stones, the towering, shapeless, twisted rocks, and sparkling sand, the nomadic Bedouins, I resonated with that fifteenth-century monk, Felix Fabri, who wrote that "every day, indeed every hour, you come into new country, of a different nature, with different conditions of atmosphere and soil, with hills of a different build and color, so that you are amazed at what you see and long for what you will see next."

And the suffering of the desert. This, too, is an important element in religious experience. By day the merciless sun from which there was no escape; by night the cutting wind from which my sleeping bag provided inadequate protection. The scarcity of water and the separation from everything that is familiar. All this creates a detachment—and detachment is basic in the religious path.

I said that environment creates religious experience. More theologically, one might say that there is a revelation of God in nature. The psalmist knew it; and, as he looked at the desert sky, he cried out: "The heavens are telling the glory of God and the firmament proclaims his handiwork" (Psalms 19:1). Paul knew it and he said that "ever since the creation of the world His invisible nature, namely, his eternal power and deity, has been clearly perceived in the things that have been made" (Romans 1:20). Yes, the vast desert reveals something of God: and it draws us into His all-pervading presence.

## II

And yet, when all is said and done, the revelation of God through the great and terrible wilderness is of secondary importance. Something more earth-shaking happened in Sinai. *God spoke.* He spoke to Moses face to face as a man might speak with his friend; and from that moment a remarkable friendship was initiated between Yahweh and the human family. From then until now "the invisible God out of the abundance of His love speaks to men as friends and lives among them."[1]

But God could have spoken elsewhere. He could have spoken in Belfast or Nagasaki. He could have spoken in Zamboanga or Kalamazoo. He chose the desert. And in subsequent Judeo-

Christian tradition the place where God spoke was called the desert. That is why the New Testament sees Jesus in the desert when he goes to a lonely place to pray, or when he climbs the mountain in Galilee, or when he walks by the sea. The Christian writers are not speaking about the physical desert with its sand and rock. For them the desert exists wherever one prays and listens to the word of God. And in our day many people find their desert in the inner city or prison or in hospital or in the plain sufferings of an ordinary life.

### III

Together with an Anglican priest friend I visited a Coptic monastery in the desert south of Alexandria. This was a new experience. For whereas Sinai and the wilderness around Jerusalem have a variety of scenery and sometimes a covering of grass which permits the pasture of flocks, this Egyptian desert consisted of sand and sand and more sand. After leaving Cairo we had gone astray, when a group of jovial monks took us into their big safari, drove us through the desert to their monastery, and treated us with royal hospitality. The monastery was like a great ship in the sea of desert, and from the roof I watched the monks like tiny ants walking out into the sand under the blazing sun. "It is our life," one monk said to me; and he explained that their life is one of presence to the desert, presence to God. For the desert is a empty and vast symbol of the unknowable God.

Again, it was an ideal setting for mysticism. The desert leads to a cosmic experience, a kenotic or emptying experience; it leads to the *nada, nada, nada* of those apophatic mystics who emphasize that we know more about what God is *not* than about what He *is*.

Yet the same question haunted me: How does this differ from the mystical experience of the Buddhist or the Hindu? How does it differ from the experience of anyone who enters the vast and lonely desert to relish the emptiness or to enter the fascinating world of supraconceptual silence? What is distinctively Christian about the prayer of these monks?

And then the answer became clear, ridiculously clear. Of course. The monks were constantly reading the Scriptures. They were attentive to the word of God. They sang His praises in liturgy. They gathered to break bread and to celebrate the new covenant in his blood. They prayed to the Virgin Mary to whom their monastery was dedicated. And when they went alone into the desert, the word was ringing in their ears and singing in their hearts. Word and sacrament carried them into the vast and empty inner desert of which the outer desert is but a symbol. Word and sacrament filled the deep, deep caverns of their unconscious minds as they walked or sat silently in those wastes of sand.

### IV

Yes, God spoke in the desert. Of course He had appeared to Abraham and revealed His name. "I appeared to Abraham, to Isaac and to Jacob, as God almighty, but by my name the Lord I did not make myself known to them" (Exodus 6:3). After revealing His name to Moses, God spoke through the prophets; and finally He spoke through His only Son. He spoke not only with words but also through mighty deeds. He spoke especially through the life, death, and resurrection of Jesus who is His only-begotten Son.

And God continues to speak. For "God who spoke of old uninterruptedly converses with the Bride of His beloved Son; and the Holy Spirit . . . leads unto all truth those who believe and makes the word of God dwell abundantly in them."[2] God continues to speak powerfully and eloquently. He carries on a conversation with the human family as He carried on a conversation with Moses. *And we hear His voice when we read the Scriptures or hear them read in community.* Listen to the Council:\*

> For in the sacred books, the Father who is in heaven meets His children with great love and speaks with them; and the force and power in the word of God is so great that it remains the support and energy of the Church, the strength of faith for her children, the food of the soul, the pure and perennial source of spiritual life.[3]

And elsewhere the same Council quotes St. Ambrose: "We speak to Him when we pray; we hear Him when we read the divine sayings."[4]

God not only spoke. He entered into covenant with His people. He called His chosen Moses to the top of the mountain and through him told the people how much He loved them, how He protected them, and He asked for their unconditional love in return. This mutual love of God and people was solemnly sealed in the blood of animals. "And Moses took the blood and threw it upon the people, and said, 'Behold the blood of the covenant which the Lord has made with you in accordance with all these words' " (Exodus 24:8). Christians believe that this covenant was renewed in the blood of Jesus who died and rose for our salvation—"he entered once and for all into the Holy Places, taking not the blood of goats and calves but his own blood, thus securing an eternal redemption" (Hebrews 9:12).

As God continues to speak, so He continues to reenact the covenant. He does so through the Eucharist wherein Christians find nourishment, receive God's love, and love God in return. Listen to the Council speaking of the two tables of word and sacrament:

> The Church has always venerated the divine Scripture just as

---

\* Throughout this book when I speak of "the Council" I mean the Second Vatican Council, 1963–1965.

she venerates the body of the Lord, since from the table of
both the word of God and the body of Christ she unceasingly
receives and offers to the faithful the bread of life, especially
in the sacred liturgy.[5]

In short, Scripture and sacrament nourish the spiritual life of all
Christians and of all Christian mystics.

Concretely, the Christian mystics have constantly read the
Scriptures and have lived the Scriptures. They quote the word
of God on every page they write. This word of Scripture has
been their nourishment and their joy. It has carried them into
the cloud of unknowing, into the silent darkness where God
dwells in inaccessible light. It has pointed the way to the deepest realm of the interior castle. "For the word of God is living
and active, sharper than any two-edged sword" (Hebrews 4:12).

Again, the Christian mystics have celebrated the Eucharist.
Those who were Catholic have believed in the real presence of
Jesus, who is the bread of life. Their interior senses have tasted
and relished this bread which, like the manna in the desert, is
sweeter than honey. They have felt the indwelling presence of
the Lord himself. And the Eucharist has united them with
Christians throughout the world.

## V

I have spoken of word and sacrament as chief nourishers
of the mystical life. Let me now mention one more source of
nourishment, namely, the word of God as it lives in the community, particularly as it lives in the masses of the people united
with their shepherds. Let me explain.

The living word of Jesus was transmitted to those disciples
who lived with him and loved him. They, in turn, passed it on
to others, and others to others, and so on. They wrote it down
(and this is Scripture) but it also passed on orally. And so it
continues to live in the people. It lives actively not only in the

hearts of bishops and theologians but also in the masses—in the hearts of the butcher, the baker, and the candlestick-maker. The old theologians expressed this in a number of Latin tags which are profoundly meaningful. *Vox populi: vox Dei*, they said, indicating that the voice of the people is the voice of God. Again, they set great store by the praying church *(ecclesia orans)* claiming that the prayer of the people is a norm of belief; *lex orandi: lex credendi*. Again, they spoke of the *sensus fidelium* (the sense of the faithful) reminding us that the faithful everywhere have a sensitivity to the word and are guided by the Spirit.

And so the mystics remain in touch with this living community and vivify it. They are never isolated—out on a limb—but part of a vibrant tradition from which they get help and guidance and to which they give support. They read the books that this tradition has produced or (for some mystics are illiterate) they receive guidance from representatives of this tradition. However deeply they penetrate into the desert, they are never alone. The support of the Christian community is always with them.

## VI

I said I was searching for the roots of Christian mysticism. Now I say unhesitatingly that there are three sources of Christian mystical experience: (1) the Word of God in sacred scripture, (2) the sacraments, particularly the Eucharist, and (3) the Word of God in the community called church.

If, then, you ask for practical advice on how to enter the Christian mystical life, I do not advise you to take the plane to Tel Aviv and the bus to the Judean desert. I do not tell you to travel to Cairo and then to Sinai or to the desert south of Alexandria. I do not tell you to sit in the lotus and breathe from your abdomen. All this is good, very good, but in the end peripheral. Instead I say:

Listen to the word! Read the Scriptures! Read them again and again with faith and love until the word comes to life within you, penetrating the deepest layers of your unconscious.

Again, celebrate the Eucharist! Break bread with the community! Be present to the mystery of faith and partake of the bread of life. This will lead you into that rich inner desert of silence and joy where your life lies hidden with Christ in God. This will lead you to say with Paul: "It is no longer I who live, but Christ lives in me" (Galatians 2:20). This will lead you to cry out with Jesus: "Abba, Father!"

Again, listen to the community. Be part of the community. Get guidance from some representative of the community; read the mystical literature the community has produced. Never get isolated. Never go out on a limb. Community!

### VII

I hear you say: "Yes, you are talking about Christian revelation. You are simply saying that Christian mysticism is rooted in the Christian revelation and that this is its unique and special dimension. Fine! Wonderful! I buy all this. But I have a difficulty: If my prayer is filled with Scripture and sacrament will it not be wordy, conceptual, discursive? Where will be the cloud of unknowing, the emptiness, the void, the silence, the altered state of consciousness? Where will be those levels of awareness which I associate with mysticism?"

I hear you. But listen to me. If you constantly receive the Eucharist and if you constantly read the Scriptures with faith, you will find that you are carried into the cloud of unknowing and the silence and the void. You will find that you are carried beyond the words to the Reality, the mysterious Reality, to which the words point. You will find that you are not just understanding the Scriptures, you are also loving them, and understanding them through love. Then the word of God will come to life in you. And this is Christian mysticism. *The Christian mystic is one who lives the Christ-mystery and is transformed by it.* He or she is one who not only knows Jesus but loves Jesus, identifies with Jesus, lives the very life of Jesus, and cries out: "Abba, Father!"

## NOTES

1. *Dei Verbum* C.1; *The Documents of Vatican II*, ed. Walter M. Abbott (New York: America Press, 1966), p. 112.
2. Ibid., C.2; ibid., p. 116.
3. Ibid., C.6; ibid., p. 125.
4. Ibid.; ibid., p. 127.
5. Ibid.; ibid., p. 125.

# 2

# Christian Mysticism

## I

I have said that I was searching for the roots of Christian mysticism. And, of course, this brings me up against the awful problem of saying what I mean by the word *mysticism*. In a former book entitled *The Inner Eye of Love*, I tried to say that mysticism is a profoundly human phenomenon appearing in more or less similar form in all the great religions. For every religion has its mystics. Let me briefly summarize what I said there.

There exists in this poor world of ours an unconditional, unrestricted love: a love that goes on and on and on, a love to which there are no limits. Just as the human mind asks questions, questions, questions, so the human heart longs to love and to love and to love. In the Christian view, however, this love is not something one drums up by personal effort. It is called forth by God Who takes the initiative. "We love because He first loved us" (1 John 4:19).

Now love is a powerful lamp, a burning candle. It throws light on its environs and leads to knowledge. This knowledge I call faith: it is the richest wisdom. And as faith penetrates deeper and deeper into the human psyche, it leads to altered states of consciousness and greatly enhanced awareness. It holds sway at the depths of one's being. And now I call it mysticism. I believe that this mysticism is found everywhere and that it exists even in those religions which do not speak of love but which demand a total commitment.

I still hold the view expressed in my former book. However, as my reader will observe, in an effort to find common ground with other religions, I approached the problem from a subjective standpoint. And since the human psyche is everywhere the same, I had no difficulty in finding a common pattern of religious experience. But in this book, which aims at highlighting what is unique and distinctive in Christian mysticism, I want to look also at the objective dimension.

"Objective dimension!" you say. "How can mystical experience have an objective dimension? Surely we call mysticism nonobjective prayer precisely because we are so united with God that subject-object distinctions disappear. The mystics say they are immersed in God like a drop of water in the ocean or like the light shining through a pane of glass. And quite apart from the mystics, some philosophers maintain that God is not an object."

I hear you. And first let me concede that much depends on what we mean by the word *object*. If by *object* we mean something "out there," something opposite to me in a dualistic sense, then God is not an object. I can never say, "God is there and I am here," as if I were separated from my Source. For God is the core of my being and the core of all beings. He is closer to me than I am to myself.

But the word *object* can be understood in another way. If I ask questions, I intend something. If I am committed, I am committed to some ideal. If I love, I love some reality. In all these cases I transcend myself, reaching out towards a reality beyond my consciousness. Or again, when I cry out: "Abba, Father!" am I not calling on a Being beyond myself, a Being who can be called *object?*"

As for the mystics, their language is full of paradox. It is true that they talk of an extraordinarily close union. The author of *The Cloud* says that *God is my being*—and that is good theology. But he never says, *I am God.* Other mystics speak constantly of a sense of presence, a sense of absence, a sense of otherness. They call on a God Who is beyond them. Those who were theologians spoke of a substantial union which never happens— because this would mean that we become the substance of God —and of a transforming union which happens in mystical experience and is union through love. All in all, if we are to avoid pantheism, we have to recognize a certain objectivity in mystical experience.

## II

Excellent studies have now been done on the origins of the word *mysticism.* The distinguished French scholar, Louis Bouyer, points out that while the words *mystery* and *mystical* were used by the Greeks to describe the rites of their mystery religions, early Christian writers used these words in their own distinct and unique way.[1] Just as the Greek *theos* and the Latin *deus,* which the Greeks and Romans used for their gods and goddesses, were applied by Christians to the God of Abraham and Isaac and Jacob and, in consequence, were totally trans- formed, so *the church fathers took the noun* mystery *and the adjec- tive* mystical *and applied them to the mystery of Christ, particularly as it appears in St. Paul.* Indeed, for the fathers, this Pauline mystery was a key to the understanding of the whole New Tes- tament. It is also the key to the understanding of Christian mysticism. For the object of Christian mysticism is precisely this mystery.

Recall those powerful passages where Paul speaks to the Corinthians about the mystery of Christ, the mystery of the cross—"a stumbling block to Jews and folly to gentiles, but to those who are called, both Jews and Greeks, Christ the power of God and the wisdom of God" (1 Corinthians 1:24). Paul imparts "a secret and hidden wisdom of God, which God desired before the ages for our glorification" (1 Corinthians 2:7). It is a knowledge taught by the Spirit and it is primarily a paradoxical understanding of the death and resurrection of Jesus.

And Colossians and Ephesians speak of the same mystery— "the mystery hidden for ages and generations and now made manifest to his saints" (Colossians 1:26). And this mystery is "Christ in you, the hope of glory" (Colossians 1:27). This is Jesus Christ in whom "the whole fullness of deity dwells bodily" (Colossians 2:9). This is the Jesus Christ whose love is unfathomable, so that Paul prays "that you, being rooted and grounded in love, may have power to comprehend with all the saints what is the breadth and length and height and depth and to know the love of Christ which surpasses knowledge, that you may be filled with all the fullness of God" (Ephesians 3:17–18). Such is the incomprehensible mystery of Christ through whom the Father wishes "to reconcile to himself all things, whether on earth or in heaven, making peace by the blood of his cross" (Colossians 1:20).

And to enter into the mystery of Christ is to approach the Father towards whom Jesus always points, and to cry out: "Abba, Father!" To enter into the mystery of Christ is to enter into the cloud of unknowing where one meets the Father in darkness and speaks to Him as one might speak with a friend. To enter into the mystery of Christ is to enter into the Trinity where, identified with Jesus and filled with the Spirit, I am one with the Father. But why say more? The whole New Testament is a record of mystery: the mystery of Jesus—"But who do you say that I am?" (Mark 16:15). The mystery of the kingdom hidden in parables. The mystery of the Father hidden in Jesus— "He who has seen me has seen the Father" (John 14:9). The mystery of the sending of the Spirit. And the eschatological mystery of the end of time—"In that day you will know that I am in my father and you in me and I in you" (John 14:20). What a series of mysteries! Christianity is basically mystery. And all is contained in the mystery of Christ. One who enters deeply into this mystery enters into mystical experience.

And do not think that to enter the mystery of Christ is to escape from the world. Again I say that the mystery of Christ is centered on his cross. This means that it is the mystery of the poor, the sick, the afflicted, the deranged, the imprisoned, the dying, and all those suffering people with whom Jesus identifies. It is the mystery of the exploited, the manipulated, the terrorized, the oppressed. It is the mystery of nuclear war, of hunger, of injustice, of human anguish. It is the mystery of you and me when we suffer and when we sin. Christian mystical experience, far from flying from the suffering and sinful world, is an entrance into its very heart.

### III

And throughout the centuries the mystery of Christ has always been the object of Christian prayer and worship, finding expression in rich and varied symbols. One such symbol is the Sacred Heart of Jesus. Pierced with a lance and pouring blood and water, the heart of Jesus has been a powerful symbol of the interior life of Jesus and of his immense love for the Father and for the human family. Entrance into the heart of Jesus means entrance not only into the mystery of Jesus himself but into the mystery of the Father whom he reveals. It means entrance not only into the suffering of Jesus himself but into the suffering of the whole land which he loves.

As the epigraph of this book I have chosen yet another symbol from St. John of the Cross: the wounded stag. In his great poem "The Spiritual Canticle" the saint writes:

> The wounded stag appears on the hill.[2]

And in his commentary the poet tells us that the wounded stag is Jesus himself. He is wounded because we are wounded. He is wounded with love. The Spanish mystic goes on to tell us that it is characteristic of the stag to climb to high places and, when wounded, to race in search of refreshment and cool water. If he hears the cry of his mate and senses that she is wounded, he immediately runs to her to embrace and comfort her. Of Jesus, the wounded stag, St. John of the Cross writes:

> Beholding that the bride is wounded with love for Him, He also, because of her moan, is wounded with love for her. Among lovers, the wound of one is a wound for both, and the two have one feeling.[3]

I have chosen this symbol for my epigraph because it shows that all Christian mysticism has its origin not in our love for Jesus but in the mystery of his great love for us. "Greater love has no man than this" (John 15:13).

Put in a nutshell, the mystery of Christ is the mystery of love. It finds powerful expression in the Johannine sentence that "God is love" (1 John 4:16). Or again it finds moving expression in the Johannine statement that "God so loved the world that He gave His only Son . . ." (John 3:16). Christian mysticism is nothing other than an entrance into the baffling mystery of love and the experience of its transforming power.

But where is this mystery of love? What signposts point to it? Where is the path?

IV

With an impressive array of quotations from the church fathers, Bouyer claims that the word *mystical* was used principally in a scriptural and sacramental context. Origen (c. 184–253), for example, looks at biblical interpretation as a religious experience and a mystical experience. A fifth-century epistle of St. Nilus (died c. 430) says that the Eucharist must be approached "not as simple bread but as mystical bread." And Theodoret (c. 393–466) calls the moment of communion "the mystical moment in which we receive the body of the Bridegroom."

My reader will observe that Bouyer's studies lead to the very conclusion I reached in the last chapter: *the pillars of Christian mysticism are word and sacrament.* It is precisely by hearing the word and participating in the sacraments, particularly the Eucharist, that I am drawn into the mystery of Christ and into the mystical life. Moreover, word and sacrament form liturgy and community. Mysticism has a strong communal dimension.

V

With Dionysius in the sixth century we find the word *mystical* applied to a very clear-cut phenomenon. In his *Theologia Mystica* Dionysius describes Moses climbing the mountain and entering into the darkness. This Dionysian darkness is what we would now call an altered state of consciousness. It is the state of a mind emptied of discursive and conceptual thinking and remaining silent and empty.

In clearly emphasizing the subjective and psychological dimension of mystical experience, Dionysius was something of an innovator. But he never rejected tradition. His *Theologia Mystica* is profoundly influenced by Gregory of Nyssa's *Life of Moses* and by Origen's *Homilies on the Exodus*. For him the darkness of the cloud of unknowing is nothing other than the mystery of

Christ, for "he transposes into the language of his own era the universal reconciliation and restoration in Christ which St. Paul preached as 'the mystery.'"[4] Dionysius stands in the full stream of biblical and eucharistic mysticism.

And succeeding ages, while retaining the scriptural and eucharistic dimensions, continued to map out the mystical states of consciousness. This was completely necessary for the spiritual guidance of timid (and less timid) mystics who walked this perilous path. One map describes the journey in terms of the purgative, illuminative, and unitive ways. Yet another, the map of the great Teresa, depicts the interior castle with seven mansions representing seven states of consciousness. A scholastic model speaks of acquired and infused contemplation. Others speak of the way of beginners, proficients, and perfect. The various states of consciousness, however, are not clear-cut. Teresa says that one may roam from mansion to mansion with great freedom.

I have said that these maps were necessary for the guidance of mystics. All the more so since not all mystical states are delectable. Some are filled with anguish and pain; some are turbulent and stormy; some are described in terms of dereliction and abandonment. Some are even dangerous and treacherous and are called "false mysticism"—not because the state itself is false but because it leads in the wrong direction and may bring the hapless mystic to destruction.

Then there was mystical theology. This was supraconceptual knowledge of the mystery. Today we think of theology in rational and scientific terms. But for Dionysius mystical theology is the hidden or secret wisdom found in deep prayer. Indeed, his mystical theology corresponds to what today we call mysticism or mystical experience. And this understanding of mystical theology is found in St. John of the Cross. About an updated mystical theology I have spoken elsewhere, maintaining that today we must elaborate a mystical theology which is nothing other than *reflection on mystical experience.*[5]

## VI

From what I have said it will be clear that *mysticism* is an orthodox Christian word, traditional, meaningful, and valuable. It will also be clear that mystical experience in its origins is thoroughly Christian, biblical, sacramental, and communitarian. Some nineteenth-century scholars, however, tried to debunk both the word and the phenomenon. Some Christian scholars saw mysticism as a pagan leprosy, a neoplatonic contamination poisoning the pure and limpid waters of biblical spirituality. Bouyer claims that much of this comes from bad scholarship. "Much verbiage would have been avoided, in this field as in many others, if students had begun by examining the texts, all the texts, in which the word occurs in ancient times, and by seeking, according to the context and not in accordance with *a priori* theories, the meaning of the word."[6]

Contemporary thought is in danger of misunderstanding mysticism in another way. Fascinated by psychology, many people identify mystical experience with the altered state of consciousness, be it ecstasy or trance or some lesser form of inner union. This is a snare. For the fact is that most of these altered states can be reproduced in the laboratory through hypnosis or biofeedback or the use of drugs or psychological techniques. What makes mysticism to be mysticism is not the altered state of consciousness but the unrestricted love, the total commitment, the enlightened faith. *What makes Christian mysticism to be Christian mysticism is the orientation to the mystery of Christ in a scriptural and sacramental context.* Assuredly the radical and loving commitment to Christ in his mysteries ordinarily leads to altered states of consciousness. But these are of secondary importance.

Besides, the act of love by which one cries out, "Abba, Father!" can arise at any level of consciousness.

Yet it is good that the study of mystical states of consciousness goes on. Great progress has been made in our day, thanks to modern psychology and to Asian religious experience. I write these lines in the Philippines where I have come in contact with many forms of trance, shamanistic in origin but now thoroughly Christianized. I believe that the ongoing study of such phenomena will help us purify our mystical theology and our understanding of the ways of God.

## VII

And so the task confronting Christianity today is to renew its mystical life. Anyone aware of the signs of the times must see a longing for deep prayer, for mystical prayer, throughout the Christian world. If we can see mysticism as a total commitment to the first precept of the Decalogue to love God with one's whole heart and soul and mind and strength; if we can see it as a commitment to the mystery of Christ; if we can see it as a transforming experience whereby one comes to love Christ in the poor and the oppressed and the despised; if we see mysticism as a road, perhaps the only road, to a total and suprarational commitment to peace; then we will realize that mystical experience is at the very core of our Christian life, the path to which all Christians are called.

Let us carry out this mystical renewal in an ecumenical context. This is a field wherein we need collaboration from Christians of all denominations. While it is true that Protestant scholars led the antimystical crusade within Christianity, it is also true that there is profound biblical mysticism within Protestantism. Indeed the lives and writings of some of the reformers are full of mysticism.

Together we can answer the longings of the people for mystical prayer. Together we can dialogue with the great mystics of Asia. This is the way of the future.

I hear you say: "I like what you say about the mystery of Christ as the unique and special dimension of Christian mysticism. This surely rings true. But I still have a question. You have spoken eloquently and written beautifully about dialogue with Buddhism. You have said that we must join with men and women of other faiths in a common search for truth. And now, by stressing the mystery of Christ, you are widening the gap that separates us from these people. How come?"

Far be it from me to do such a thing. I cannot believe that entrance into the mystery of Christ separates me from any human person in the whole wide world. Let me again quote the Council. It is saying that God's grace is at work in all human hearts and that by his Incarnation the Son of God has united himself in some fashion with every man and woman; and then with delicacy and grace it continues:

> For since Christ died for all, and since our ultimate vocation is in fact one, and divine, we ought to believe that the Holy Spirit in a manner known only to God offers to every man and woman the possibility of being associated with this paschal mystery.[7]

Everyone has the possibility of entering into the mystery of Christ. Everyone is loved by the wounded stag. Are we not all—Buddhists, Christians and everyone else—faced with the same mystery hidden from all ages and now revealed through Jesus Christ in the fullness of time?

## NOTES

1. See Louis Bouyer, "Mysticism: An Essay on the History of the Word," in *Understanding Mysticism*, ed. Richard Woods (New York: Doubleday, 1980), pp. 42–

55. See also Louis Bouyer, *The Spirituality of the New Testament and the Fathers* (London: Burns and Oates, 1963).

2. "The Spiritual Canticle," Stanza 13, n.9, in *The Collected Works of St. John of the Cross,* trans. Kieran Kavanaugh and Otilio Rodriguez (Washington, D.C.: ICS Publications, 1979), p. 411.

3. Ibid., p. 460.

4. Bouyer, "Mysticism: An Essay on the History of the Word."

5. See in my book, *The Inner Eye of Love* (San Francisco: Harper & Row; London: Collins, 1978), chap. 4, "Mystical Theology."

6. Bouyer, "Mysticism: An Essay on the History of the Word."

7. *Gaudium et Spes* C.1, 122; *The Documents of Vatican II,* ed. Walter M. Abbot (New York: American Press, 1966), pp. 221–222.

# 3

# Moses the Mystic

## I

At 4:30 A.M. on a bitterly cold April morning, we the scholars (smile) climbed into a big, open safari and headed for Sinai. Sleepy, silent, wrapped in overcoats, balaclava helmets, and a variety of contraptions, we huddled together for protection against the piercing, desert wind. Skirting Jerusalem, our safari went down, down, down that winding road past the inn of the Good Samaritan—down to sea level, below sea level, down to the Dead Sea. And now we began to thaw out, to get rid of those overcoats, and to relish the warm air. Finally, at 'En Gedi we uncorked our flasks and indulged in hot coffee. We were close to the lovers' cave: "Return, return, O Shulammite, return, return, that we may look upon you" (Song of Songs 6:13).

Beside me sat a young scholar who was writing a commentary on Exodus. I asked him what he thought of Moses the mystic. "Moses the mystic!" he gasped. "We've just about reached belief in the historical existence of Moses. Whether he was a Jew or an Egyptian we do not know. Whether there was one exodus or a series of migrations we do not know. What route the Israelites took we do not know. Whether Moses met the real Pharaoh, or some lesser light we do not know. We know so little! How can you talk about Moses the mystic?"

I explained my point: "The church fathers and the desert fathers read Exodus as a story. They read and reread. They heard it proclaimed at liturgy. They relished its words and phrases in their *lectio divina*. And they identified with Moses. With him they climbed the mountain and entered the cloud. With him they spoke to God face to face as one might speak with a friend. *And they found that they were drawn into the mystical life.* In this sense Moses was a mystic."

"I could not quarrel with that," he answered. And we remained friends.

In fact we had touched upon one of the most thorny theological problems of our day, or of any day: How interpret the Scriptures?

It is now clear to everybody that the historical-critical approach, however valuable, is woefully insufficient. It alone will not put us in touch with the underlying mystery; it alone will not bring us to those eternal realities towards which the Scriptures point; it alone will not enrich our lives with mysticism. How, then, are we to approach and interpret the Scriptures?

About this I have written at length elsewhere and need not repeat myself here.[1] Only let me make two points.

The first is that in addition to the knowledge which comes from science there is a knowledge which comes from love—love for the sacred text, love for the human authors, unrestricted love for the Divine Author. This love leads to involvement, to union, to enlightenment, to conversion of heart. United with the text, I come to live it and to understand it *through life*. This is the knowledge that Aquinas calls *knowledge of connaturality*. It is wonderfully high wisdom. It is mystical wisdom. To compare the knowledge coming from science with the knowledge coming from love is like comparing the light of a candle with the light of the sun. Yet both forms of knowledge are necessary.

My second point is that the Council, calling on an ancient

Christian tradition, claims that the new Testament is hidden in the Old and that the Old is made manifest in the New. Here are the Council's words:

> God, the inspirer and author of both testaments, wisely arranged that the New Testament be hidden in the Old and the Old be made manifest in the New . . . the books of the Old Testament with all their parts, caught up into the proclamation of the gospel, acquire and show forth their full meaning in the New Testament and in turn shed light on it and explain it.[2]

With this in mind we can see how Gregory of Nyssa, Dionysius, and the rest see Moses climbing the mountain as *entering into the mystery of Christ.* We can also see how Christian mystical writers from Augustine to the author of *The Cloud* and from Origen to Thomas Aquinas have seen Moses as the model of mystical prayer. These authors have seen the cloud of Exodus as a symbol of that supraconceptual obscurity into which the mystic necessarily enters. They have seen all those symbols—the wilderness, the burning bush, the cloud, the pillar of fire, the paschal lamb, the water from the rock, the manna, the golden calf, the tabernacle, the ark of the covenant—as expressing different aspects of the Christ-mystery.

Let me, then, following in the footsteps of those mystical giants, humbly pay tribute to Moses the mystic.

## II

The mystical life sometimes begins with an overpowering and unforgettable experience of God's loving presence. Such was the case with the prophets who saw God in an inaugural vision. Such was the case with Paul who met Jesus on the road to Damascus. Such was the case with Moses to whom the angel of the Lord appeared in a flame of fire out of the midst of a bush. God is present, tangibly present. This is the God of Abraham, the God of Isaac, the God of Jacob. This is the transcendent God. But now He is very, very close. Moses takes off his shoes because the ground is holy. "And Moses hid his face, for he was afraid to look at God" (Exodus 3:6).

Ordinary fire consumes and reduces to ashes. But this fire of God's presence destroys nothing. It gives life; and out of the bush Moses hears himself called by name: "Moses, Moses!" He is uniquely loved and specially chosen.

And as Moses has a name, so also has God. "I am who I am"; or "I am" or "I will be what I will be" or "I will cause to be what I will cause to be." Whatever our interpretation, we cannot avoid the note of *presence, loving presence.* "I am presence," says God.

Nor is this presence static. It is a dynamic presence, a guiding presence; and Yahweh subsequently assures Moses; "My presence will go with you and I will give you rest" (Exodus 33:14). This presence guides Moses and the people through the wilderness as a cloud by day and a pillar of fire by night. "And the Lord went before them by day in a pillar of cloud to lead them along the way, and by night in a pillar of fire to give them light, that they might travel by day and by night" (Exodus 13:21). This presence gives courage, joy, self-confidence, energy, power. When Moses stammers and stumbles and balks at the magnitude of the mission, the voice assures him: "But I will be with you . . ." (Exodus 3:12).

Now all this symbolism accurately describes the mystical life of thousands of Christians. Their mystical journey has begun with an obscure sense of presence, a conviction that God is close. He is around me and within me, without being identical with me. And as time goes on, I may reach the conviction (either gradually or in a flash) that I am loved and chosen—that I am called by name as was Moses. Not that my name is audibly called. More often an inner *silent voice* assures me of a deeply personal, loving call. This is a source of great joy and unshakable confidence: it carries an inner authority and I cannot disobey.

Again, this presence of God is dynamic, leading me like the cloud by day and the pillar of fire by night. With this as my guide I no longer reason or think or calculate. Such thinking and calculation would be a subtle snare distracting me from the deeper promptings of the Spirit.

St. John of the Cross, writing about the obscure night (which is his cloud), sings out:

> O guiding light!
> O night more lovely than the dawn![3]

And, wonder of wonders, the night guides, with more certainty than the noonday sun, to the union of lover and beloved:

> O night that has united
> The Lover with His beloved,
> Transforming the beloved in her Lover.[4]

How wonderfully the presence of the Lord guides us through the desert of life to the promised land, which is loving union with Him!

Admittedly, the notion of a guiding night is paradoxical. How can the darkness guide? The other symbol, the pillar of fire, is easier to grasp. Interiorized, this pillar of fire becomes *the living flame of love* burning brightly within the breast of the mystic. The mystical life finally consists in fidelity to this inner fire glowing gently in my heart. It tells me what to do and where to go. It guides me unerringly through the desert of life to the promised land where dwells the One I love.

And in all this, the unique dimension of the Judeo-Christian tradition shines forth. Moses himself claims that he and his people are unique precisely because the presence of God goes with them always:

> For how shall it be known that I have found favor in thy sight, I and thy people? Is it not in thy going with us, so that we are distinct, I and thy people, from all other people, that are upon the face of the earth? [Exodus 33:16]

This guiding presence is indeed a distinct characteristic of the Judeo-Christian mystical journey.

## III

Central to the mystical life of Moses is his friendship with God. "Thus the Lord used to speak to Moses face to face, as a man speaks with his friend" (Exodus 33:11). To Jew and Gentile it is indeed a mind-boggling thing that the omnipotent God should speak to puny men and women as a friend. Yet the theme of intimacy with God runs all through the Bible, reaching a touching climax with the words of Jesus to his disciples: "You are my friends . . ." (John 15:14).

The intimacy of Moses with God is very real. He complains to Yahweh, argues with Him, pours forth his frustrations, intercedes for the people, makes the audacious request to see the face of God. What intimacy is here! And Moses always prefaces his remarks with the words: "If I have found favor in your sight . . ."; as if to say, "If you really love me, and I know that you do . . ." Think of his anguished struggle with God when, in spite of all those plagues, Pharaoh's heart remained obdurate. Think of that passage in Numbers where Moses identifies with his own femininity, assumes the role of the mother and exclaims:

> Did I conceive all this people? Did I bring them forth, that thou shouldst say to me: "Carry them in your bosom as a nurse carries the sucking child . . . ?" [Numbers 11:12]

Only close friends talk like that.

And again, the mystical life of numerous Christians can be described in terms of friendship. In her inimitable, homely way, St. Teresa can say that "prayer is nothing else than an intimate friendship, a frequent heart-to-heart conversation with him whom we know loves us." And many Christians, following her example, can sit in the presence of God and talk to Him as a friend. Like Moses they speak about their problems, air their frustrations, make audacious petitions, intercede for their families, all the time realizing that they are loved by the friend of friends. Here is a wonderful model of prayer.

"Prayer," you say, "Yes. But is it mystical prayer? Surely mystical prayer is silent, wordless in a cloud of unknowing."

Let me pause a moment. Words can come from various levels of the psyche; and mystical words come from the deepest level of all. While it is true that mystical prayer contains periods of wordlessness, it is also true that there can be mystical dialogue, mystical conversation, rising up from an altered state of consciousness, from those hidden depths where God dwells in inaccessible light. Nor are these words necessarily earth-shaking and ecstatic. They may be simple and quiet like the words of one who speaks face to face with a friend. Such were the words of Moses. Such are the words of innumerable Christian mystics.[5]

## IV

As the story of Moses the mystic entered the mystical literature of Christianity, the question was asked: Did Moses see God? In the terminology of the scholastic theologians: Did Moses attain to the beatific vision in this life? Did he see the essence of God? While we can all see God *as He is in creatures*, did Moses see God *as He is in Himself*? And as the question was asked about Moses, so also it was asked about St. Paul. Remember that in The Second Epistle to the Corinthians Paul says that

he was caught up to the third heaven—and, indeed, to paradise. Does this mean that Paul also enjoyed the vision of God's
essence? And if Moses and Paul saw God, what about the host
of other holy men and women, beginning with Elias?

A solid theological tradition, rooted in Exodus itself, states
unhesitatingly that Moses did not see God. His audacious prayer
to see God's glory meets with a clear-cut refusal:

> I will make all my goodness pass before you and will proclaim
> before you my name. . . . But . . . you cannot see my face; for
> man shall not see me and live." [Exodus 33:19–20]

The Lord then comes down in a cloud; Moses is filled with awe
as the Lord passes before him; but the face of God he does not
see. And this scene finds an echo in the fourth gospel which
firmly declares that "no one has ever seen God . . ." (John 1:
18). This is clear speaking.

In his excellent study, *Western Mysticism*, Edward Cuthbert
Butler, with ample quotations from the fathers, maintains that
the tradition that neither Moses nor anyone else sees the face of
God is firmly grounded throughout Christian theology. However, the other theory, that Moses and Paul enjoyed a fleeting
vision of God, is found in Augustine and Thomas, mighty and
prestigious theological giants. Augustine based his claim principally on the text of Numbers that God spoke to Moses "mouth
to mouth":

> If there is a prophet among you, I the Lord make myself
> known to him in a vision, I speak with him in a dream. Not
> so with my servant Moses. . . . With him I speak mouth to
> mouth, clearly, and not in dark speech; and he beholds the
> form of the Lord. [Numbers 12:6]

Edward Cuthbert Butler rightly says that this text (like the others stating that God spoke to Moses face to face) says nothing
about the beatific vision. As for Paul, he nowhere claims to

have seen God. Butler, claiming that Thomas followed Augustine, concludes:

> In the face of . . . biblical evidence, and of the grave philosophical difficulties involved, it may well be thought that but for St. Augustine's ill-founded speculation, accepted and endorsed by St. Thomas, the idea of the vision of God's essence by any man would not have found a place in theological tradition.[6]

Alas, Augustine and Thomas were not familiar with the historical-critical method. Their ill-founded speculation reminds us that science plays a vital role in the interpretation of Scripture.

But a problem remains. Granted that Moses did not see God, what was the nature of his experience?

The old theologians were fascinated by the picture of Moses entering the darkness. Remember how God came down in a thick cloud. Sinai was wrapped in smoke. "And the people stood afar off, while Moses drew near to the thick darkness where God was" (Exodus 20:21).

In his *Life of Moses*, Gregory of Nyssa, watching Moses enter the thick darkness, claims that the great leader did have a direct vision of God. But (paradox of paradoxes) it was a dark vision. It was a seeing which is not seeing, a knowledge which is ignorance. Graphically he describes how the mind (the mind of Moses or the mind of any mystic) travels beyond all sensible seeing, beyond all imaginative seeing, beyond all understanding and reasoning until it *sees God in darkness*. Here are his words:

> For leaving behind everything that is observed, not only what sense comprehends but also what the intelligence thinks it sees, it keeps on penetrating deeper until by the intelligence's yearning for understanding it gains access to the invisible and the incomprehensible, and then it sees God. This is the true

knowledge of what is sought; this is the seeing that consists in not seeing, because that which is sought transcends all knowledge, being separated on all sides by incomprehensibility as by a kind of darkness.[7]

Gregory has been called "the father of Christian mysticism" and this passage was to have immense influence on subsequent apophatic mysticism and its offspring, the theology of negation.

St. John of the Cross follows in the footsteps of Gregory and of Gregory's disciple Dionysius. Put briefly, his doctrine of the darkness is as follows: God is so utterly different from anything or anyone we know, the love of God is so different from anything we have ever experienced, the glory of God is such a dazzling and blinding light, that as we approach God our dazed faculties, unable to endure the sight, are plunged into the most radical darkness. Just as the bat is blinded by the intense light of the sun, so we are blinded by the intense light of God. We do have a vision of God (as Moses had a vision of God) but we see Him in darkness. *We see Him through faith.* St. John of the Cross elaborates a profound theology of faith in which he does not hesitate to say that by faith we meet God face to face. And in naked faith this dark vision of God is filled with mystical suffering.

Faith is a dark, dark vision of God. To this I shall return. Here it is enough to watch Moses enter the cloud, recalling that he is followed by a host of mystics who enter the darkness where God resides in light inaccessible.

V

Moses is indeed a rich and many-sided personality. Sometimes he is depicted as a prophet. And a great prophet he was: "And there has not arisen a prophet since in Israel like Moses, whom the Lord knew face to face . . ." (Deuteronomy

34:10). But the prophecy of Moses came out of his mystical experience and was its fruit.

Again, Moses is sometimes called the lawgiver. And a great lawgiver he was—immortalized in marble by Michelangelo. Yet the law came out of his mystical meeting with God.

Again, Moses was the leader of his people, the former of community. But he can weld the people together only because he has met God in mystical prayer.

And through Exodus we see him grow. We see him transfigured. This young Hebrew who killed the Egyptian and hid him in the sand; this young Hebrew who stammered so much that he needed help from Aaron; this young Hebrew is so transformed through mystical encounter that his face shines with a blinding radiance—with the glory of that God Who spoke to him as a friend. "And when Aaron and all the people of Israel saw Moses, behold, the skin of his face shone, and they were afraid to come near him" (Exodus 24:30). Mystical love has transformed not only his mind and heart but his very body and his whole person.

And the mystical experience of Moses was not just his own. It was the experience of the whole people of Israel; for they (in Paul's enigmatic phrase) "were baptized into Moses in the cloud in the sea" (1 Corinthians 10:2). Just as John was the beloved disciple and we are all beloved disciples, so Moses was the friend of God and we are all friends of God. As Moses was the mystic, so we are all called to be mystics. We also can climb the mountain where God will speak to us face to face as one speaks to a friend.

### NOTES

1. See in my book, *The Mirror Mind* (New York: Harper & Row; London: Collins, 1981), chap. 5, "The Holy Books."

2. *Dei Verbum*, C.4,16; *The Documents of Vatican II*, ed. Walter M. Abbot (New York: American Press, 1966), p. 122.

3. *The Collected Works of St. John of the Cross*, trans. Kieran Cavanaugh and Otilio Rodriguez (Washington, D.C.: ICS Publications, 1979), p. 9.

4. Ibid.

5. *The Mirror Mind*, chap. 4, "Words and Silence."

6. Edward Cuthbert Butler, *Western Mysticism* (New York: E. P. Dutton, 1923; London: Constable, 1926), pp. 53, 54.

7. Gregory of Nyssa, *The Life of Moses*, trans. Abraham J. Malherbe and Everett Ferguson (New York: Paulist Press, 1978).

# 4

# Presence and Absence (1)

I

I have said that the Book of Exodus is pervaded with the sense of God's presence and can be read as a great treatise on mysticism. I have spoken about Moses the mystic, Moses the friend of God. And now I would like to speak about the sense of presence and absence in the lives of millions of Christians who, following in the footsteps of Moses, have enjoyed friendship with their God.

II

From the earliest times, Christians who wish to come close to God have been urged to walk constantly in His loving presence. We have been urged to reflect that God is everywhere; for He is the great reality in whom we live and move and have our being. Is not this the message of the Book of Psalms which poetically reminds us of the all-pervading presence of God? And then there is the New Testament teaching that the Blessed Trinity dwells deeply in us as in a temple. We know that St. Ignatius of Loyola told his disciples to recall the presence of God before entering into prayer; and he advised busy people to pause for a moment during the day to recall that God is close, very close, and that He is dwelling in them. Then there is the holy Carmelite, Brother Lawrence, who taught "the practice of the presence of God" as a key to the inner journey.

As we advance along the path to God, however, there comes a time when the presence of God ceases to be a *practice* and becomes a *given*. It is no longer something I *do* but something that happens. I suddenly, perhaps unexpectedly, become aware that God is here. I become aware of what the mystics call "an obscure sense of presence." It is obscure because it has no clear-cut images or pictures of God. It is memorable and important because it is an altered, new state of consciousness, an enhanced awareness as though I was entering a hitherto unfamiliar world, or as though I was suddenly in possession of a sixth sense.

This experiential sense of God's loving presence is traditionally regarded as the first stage of Christian mysticism. When it comes over me, I may have a sense of the divine indwelling, a realization that God lives at the very center of my being. Or it may be a feeling that I am surrounded by God as by a loving atmosphere, that I am plunged in God like a sponge in the ocean. Or it may simply be a sense that God is present in a way I cannot understand: I cannot locate that presence inside or outside or anywhere at all.

This sense of God's presence carries great conviction. Now I need no proof that God exists. I cannot deny it; I cannot deny my own experience; for that experience is self-authenticating. Of course my certainty is subjective. That is to say, it is for me alone. I cannot *prove* God's presence to anyone else. All I can do is bear witness to what has happened to me.

## III

This sense of presence may come at any time in life. Not infrequently children experience God's presence, only to forget about it when they grow to adulthood. In adults the same experience is often the outcome of years of discursive and ejaculatory prayer, of reading the Scriptures, and of constant celebration of the Eucharist. Their prayer has become more and more simple, more and more an activity of the heart, till the day comes when they just want to be silent and wordless in the felt presence of God. Now they no longer desire to think; they only want to be.

The sense of God's presence may be accompanied by distractions. It is as though there were two layers in the psyche. At one level the imagination is running wild: at a deeper level I am quietly aware of God's presence. In this state, technically known as *the prayer of quiet,* all good teachers recommend that one remain quietly in God's presence at the depths of one's being, making no effort to chase away the distraction. Don't fight! Let them be! Let them come and go! St. Teresa calls the wild and unruly imagination "the fool of the house."

Yet at other times one's faculties may be so held by the divine presence that one seems to be in some kind of ligature, unable to think or pray discursively. This ligature may even lead to ecstasy.

It is important to note that this presence is not static. God is not present in me like still water in a glass. No, no. The presence of God changes me radically, guiding me through the inner desert like the cloud by day and the pillar of fire by night. Of course I may be sitting in seeming passivity; I may seem to be doing nothing at all. I may have scruples that I am wasting my time. But, unknown to myself, growth is taking place. I am being changed like the log transformed into the fire. Put in scriptural terms, the presence of God is effecting in me a profound *metanoia.* "Change your hearts and believe the Gospel," said Jesus; and in the mystical life he himself is changing the heart of stone into a heart of flesh.

But not only is the heart changed by this silent contemplation. A profound change is wrought in the whole person. The
body is transformed as was the body of Moses who wore a veil
on his face to conceal the radiant beauty and splendor of God's
glory. In the same way, the contemplative becomes more and
more beautiful, more and more attractive, more and more
charming and lovable.

## IV

Interestingly enough, some of the most vivid descrip-
tions of mystical experience come from the lips of men and
women who have been recalled from the brink of death. Such
people often say that, as they slipped towards death, they
seemed to enter into a new dimension, into another ground of
being, into a state of consciousness where time and space
seemed different. The experience was not terrifying because
they were greeted by a warm and loving presence, or they
experienced an accepting light. They claim that the experience
so changed them that they returned to ordinary life liberated
from the fear of death and with a new scale of values. What had
seemed important was no longer important; what had seemed
unimportant had become the very center of their lives.

Now all this is reminiscent of the talk of the mystics. It is all
the more interesting in view of the fact that the old authors
claimed that mystical experience is a foretaste of eternal life.
What more natural than that this foretaste should come when,
faced with death, one stands at the gates of eternity?

## V

And this brings me to an issue discussed at length by
mystical theologians: Do many people enjoy the loving sense of
God's presence? How frequent is the mystical experience?

Some theologians at the beginning of the century claimed

that mysticism was a special charismatic gift granted to a privileged few. Others, holding that it was no more than a development of the ordinary grace of baptism, spoke of "the universal vocation to mysticism." Every Christian, they said, is called to be a mystic.

I myself have come to believe in the universal vocation to mysticism for the following reasons.

First, the Council spoke of the universal vocation to holiness, insisting that all the faithful are called to the summit of perfection.[1] Now it is true that the Council did not speak explicitly about mysticism. Nevertheless, if you read the relevant document you see that the Council quite forcefully rejects the medieval notion of an elite called to perfection and a riffraff called to salvation. Elitism is gone. And as we are all called to holiness, may not all be called to mysticism? And will not this be especially true if the essence of mysticism is nothing other than the unrestricted love, the agape which forms the very core of Christian holiness?

Second, if one holds with Karl Rahner that Christianity is basically presence to transcendent mystery, then the seeds of mystical presence are already in the mind and heart at baptism. And the Christian life consists in being more and more present to the mystery as the mystery is ever more lovingly present to us. Rahner himself seems to draw this conclusion when he claims that the fervent Christian of the future will be a mystic.

My third reason is personal. As my experience of the Christian world deepens, I see that many, many people are called to pray in altered states of consciousness. Here in the Philippines, where I write this book, I see simple people praying silently for hours in the great prayer centers of Quiapo and Baclaran in central Manila—and well-informed people tell me that the poor are indeed blessed with mystical gifts. And what happens here happens throughout the world. This leads me to the conclusion that the Christian spirit open to God moves spontaneously towards mystical states of consciousness. Sometimes people need only a little instruction. They need only be told to use fewer words, to be quiet, to let themselves be drawn into the cloud of unknowing.

It is true, of course, that some committed Christians seem to experience no mysticism during their lives. But we cannot exclude the possibility that for these, mystical experience comes at the time of death. For these the mystical moments of death are a preparation for the most radical, altered state, which is eternal life.

## VI

Now let me say a word about the theology of this sense of presence.

Following St. Thomas and St. John of the Cross, we can distinguish three modes of divine presence: *presence by essence, presence by grace, presence by love.*

*Presence by essence* is a consequence of ongoing creation: if God were not present, holding it in existence, the universe would immediately fall into nothingness. And the same is true for us. If God were not present, holding us in existence, we would fall into nothingness. *Presence by grace* is a consequence of baptism whereby the Blessed Trinity comes to dwell within our hearts. But we may not be aware of this divine indwelling. *Presence by love* is the existential and experiential sense of presence about which I have been speaking.

Presence through love! Remember I said that altered states of consciousness can be induced by hypnosis, by biofeedback, by drugs. Yogis enter into trance by staring at the flame of a candle or by fixing their gaze on a single point. *The special characteristic of Christian prayer is that altered states of consciousness are induced not by techniques but by love.*

Presence through love! Not my love for God but God's love for me. Or, more correctly, the intense mutual love existing between God and the human person. Usually this love is the fruit of years of toil, but sometimes it comes quite suddenly to those who reach the vineyard at the eleventh hour. It is precisely this love that creates a sense of presence (and later a sense of absence) that leads to ecstasy, that leads to forgetfulness of time, that leads to those altered states of consciousness which forever will be the subject of psychological research.

Love and presence lead to union. Again the scholastics distinguish between an *essential union* with God common to all created things, and a *transforming* union arising from love. I spoke of this when I said that God can be considered as an object. Let me now quote St. John of the Cross on how the soul is one with God yet not one with God:

> When God grants this supernatural favor to the soul, so great a union is caused that all the things of both God and the soul become one in participant transformation, and the soul appears to be God more than a soul. Indeed, it is God by participation. Yet truly, its being (even though transformed) is naturally as distinct from God's as it was before, just as the window, although illumined by the ray, has an existence distinct from the ray.[2]

Here, while stressing the most intimate union, the saint avoids any taint of pantheism.

## VII

Scholastic theologians spoke of acquired and infused presence, as they spoke of acquired and infused contemplation. Acquired contemplation is found through personal effort with the aid of ordinary grace: infused contemplation is that gift of presence that comes gratuitously and is identified with mysticism. This distinction is based on a psychology which speaks of a twofold knowledge: ordinary knowledge coming through the senses according to the Aristotelian dictum that there is nothing in the intellect which was not previously in the senses (*nihil est in intellectu quod non fuit prius in sensu*); and extraordinary or mystical knowledge directly *infused* by God who now communicates Himself by pure spirit.

I believe that today, when we use a new psychology, this distinction between acquired and infused is no longer useful. We now speak in terms of altered states of consciousness; and it is difficult to maintain that one state is more "infused by God" than the other. Indeed, we know that some people (and this is particularly true in Asia) can enter into trance with the greatest ease. And who can say that this trance-like state is more "infused" than their ordinary, waking consciousness? In other words, to call one state "acquired" and the other "infused" is highly questionable.

And yet we cannot neglect an age-old Christian tradition that God sometimes acts directly on the human soul. Listen to the author of *The Cloud* speaking about grace-filled moments when God works all by Himself:

> Then you will feel little or no constraint, for God will sometimes work in your spirit all by Himself. Yet not always nor for very long but as it seems best to Him. When He does you will rejoice and be happy to let Him do as He wishes.[3]

These are indeed special moments when one exclaims: "This is God! I cannot doubt it! I did nothing to merit this wonderful grace."

Ignatius of Loyola talks about similar experiences and he calls them moments of "consolation without previous cause." For him this consolation is of the greatest importance because here "there can be no deception . . . since it can proceed from God our Lord only."

It should be noted, however, that Ignatius and the author of *The Cloud* are not building up a psychological system in which certain states are caused by God alone. They are speaking of privileged moments when I can have *subjective certainty* that God is present and that I am personally loved by Him.

### VIII

I hear you say: "You are speaking about the presence of God. But what about Jesus Christ? Where is he in this obscure sense of presence? Where is the specifically Christian dimension you set out to explore?"

I believe that the obscure sense of presence is part of the religious experience of all the monotheistic religions. However, my Christian faith tells me that when I enter into the cloud of unknowing and experience this obscure sense of presence, I am present to the mystery of Christ—or, rather, that the mystery of Christ is present to me. Not that I have a clear-cut picture of the Risen Jesus. It is rather that I relish the presence of a mystery hidden for ages in God and revealed through Jesus Christ.

### NOTES

1. *Lumen Gentium* C.5; *The Documents of Vatican II*, ed. Walter M. Abbot (New York: American Press, 1966), p. 65ff.
2. "The Ascent of Mount Carmel," in *The Collected Works of St. John of the Cross*, trans. Kieran Kavanaugh and Otilio Rodriguez (Washington, D.C.: ICS Publications, 1979), II, 5, p. 117.
3. *The Cloud of Unknowing and The Book of Privy Counselling*, ed. and trans. William Johnston (New York: Doubleday Image Book, 1973), chap. 26, pp. 83–84.

# 5

# Presence and Absence (2)

## I

I have spoken of God's presence. He is closer to us than we are to ourselves. Above all, He is present to us by love, as we are present to Him by love. But, alas, we do not always feel His all-pervading presence. The masters agree that the mystical path has its hour of abandonment, of desolation, of darkness. These are times when God (though intimately present) seems far, far away, and we cry out: "Where are you, my God? Where have you hidden, Beloved?" Such was the cry of the psalmist who exclaimed: "My God, my God, why hast thou forsaken me?" (Psalm 22:1). And, wonder of wonders, these very words echo on the lips of Jesus: "Lama sabacthani?"

Paul, too, had his times of awful desolation: "We were so utterly, unbearably crushed that we despaired of life itself. Why, we felt we had received the sentence of death . . ." (2 Corinthians 1:8–9). What was biting Paul? What is behind the desolation, the seeming absence of God which we all experience?

One cause of desolation is simply the ordinary pain of living. We human beings cannot forever remain at a high pitch of mystical awareness. We must come down to earth. And when Paul speaks concretely of his desolation he talks about shipwrecks and hunger and thirst and sleeplessness and criticism from the brethren. All this could happen to any of us; and it would knock us into a state of desolation where we ask: Where is God? In other words, to use modern parlance, desolation has an element of humdrum anxiety, depression, insecurity, sadness, melancholy, deflation, and all the negative emotions that are part of human living.

But this is not all. Desolation and darkness belong to, are built into, the mystical process. Let me explain why.

In the mystical life the shadow part of our personality rises to the surface of consciousness. We are confronted with our own seamy side. We get into an altered state of consciousness that is very, very painful. This may take the form of fears, anxieties, neuroses, childhood traumas, hurts and wounds of the past— painful memories of all kinds. Or it may take the form of the seven deadly sins about which I shall speak in the next chapter. All this darkness floats to the surface (or, put in another way, I enter more deeply into an altered state of consciousness where I meet it) and the result is very, very painful. Some people may feel themselves filled with the black, black guilt of an Oedipus who killed his father and married his mother. Oedipus, driven to despair, gouged out his eyes in bitter self-hatred. And the mystic may feel the same despair even when he or she calls with agony on Jesus the savior. Other people may feel anxiety, scrupulosity, insecurity, doubt. They may experience the unresolved conflicts, the unfinished business of childhood—the tears not shed, the anger never released, the fear not expressed, the curiosity not satisfied. And in all this they feel lost in the storm, until Jesus comes walking on the waters to bring them peace and integration.

Here let me pause to observe that the contemplative process

has much in common with psychotherapy. In both cases one is painfully and inescapably brought face to face with one's shadow. But the mystic is healed by calling with faith on Jesus the savior. Let me further pause to state that psychologists will never understand the human psyche with all its altered states until they look carefully at the mystical journey towards wholeness. But back to my theme.

God is present in all these hurts. He is more present in darkness than in light. He is nearer in time of desolation than in time of consolation. So the concrete advice is: Stay with the darkness. Go through it. Don't run away! And through all this you will grow from childhood to maturity; for your faculties will expand, making you more and more capable of receiving those sublime communications which come from the darkness of God.

All this is the night of the senses.

The night of the spirit is concerned with meaning. Now philosophers and sages keep telling us that we are all symbolic animals and find meaning through symbols. Moreover it is precisely religion which provides the symbols we need for our spiritual nourishment—God our Father, Jesus our savior, the stories of Scripture, the story of life after death, and so on. And it may happen that as we grow in love, as our minds and hearts expand, our symbols lose meaning. They no longer talk to us about God or about anything. Only one symbol remains: emptiness, darkness, absence. A terrible night is now caused by *loss of meaning*.

One who suffered in this way was Thérèse of Lisieux (1873–1897) about whom I would now like to say a word.

Born into a pious French family, Thérèse from early childhood had no doubt that one day she would leave earth to live forever with God in heaven. "Just as the genius of Christopher Columbus gave him a presentiment of a new world when nobody even thought of such a thing, so also I felt that another land would one day serve me as a permanent dwelling place."[1] But as she matured in spirit (even though she was chronologically very young) this clear belief in another world began to fade. Like Moses she entered into a thick, thick cloud; she entered into the night of faith. Here are her poignant words:

> Then suddenly the fog which surrounds me becomes more dense; it penetrates my soul and envelops it in such a way that it is impossible to discover within it the sweet image of my fatherland; everything has disappeared! When I want to rest my heart fatigued by the darkness which surrounds it by the memory of the luminous country after which I aspire, my torment redoubles; it seems to me that the darkness, borrowing the voice of sinners, says mockingly to me: "You are dreaming about the light, about a fatherland embalmed in the sweetest perfumes; you are dreaming about the eternal possession of the Creator of all these marvels; you believe that one day you will walk out of this fog which surrounds you! Advance, advance; rejoice in death which will give you not what you hope for but a night still more profound, the night of nothingness."[2]

The fog is, of course, the cloud of unknowing. How dark it has become! It is no longer a luminous cloud but a thick night. And Thérèse writes to her Superior: "Dear Mother, the image I wanted to give you of the darkness that obscures my soul is as imperfect as a sketch is to the model; however, I don't want to write any longer about it; I fear I might blaspheme; I fear even that I have already said too much."[3]

In spite of the darkness, Thérèse continues to write and speak enthusiastically about the love of God and about His mercy. But she herself confesses:

> When I sing of the happiness of heaven and the eternal possession of God, I feel no joy in this, for I sing simply of

what *I want to believe*. It is true that at times a very small ray of the sun comes to illumine the darkness, and then the trial ceases *for an instant*, but afterwards the memory of this ray, instead of causing me joy, makes my darkness even more dense.[4]

The italics are not mine, but hers. She felt that she no longer believed in eternal life or in a transcendent God. She felt that at heart she was an atheist.

How do we explain this agonizing state of consciousness of Thérèse? We are here faced with mystery. But let me make three observations.

First, there is the paradoxical fact that the very love which in the early stages creates a warm sense of presence eventually creates a gnawing sense of absence. I have already said that love of God is so different from anything we know, so different from what we ordinarily call love, so utterly unfamiliar, that our human faculties, unable to bear the weight, are plunged into thick darkness. Face to face with God, Thérèse was blinded by the excess of light. But, alas, she was unable to understand that the blackness was a dark vision of God.

Second, the symbolism which formerly nourished her life fell to pieces. The Christian story sounded like a fairy tale. She was left with the ultimate archetype: emptiness, nothingness. And *with the loss of symbol came a loss of meaning*: she no longer saw meaning in the great story on which she had built her life.

Third, some unresolved childhood neuroses may have remained in her unconscious mind. We know that in her last months of agony she feared she might destroy herself and asked that sharp instruments not be placed within her reach. We also know that she exhibited some neurotic tendencies in childhood. Some unfinished business may have remained—some vestiges of unresolved conflict. If this is so, the night of sense and the night of spirit came together. And what thick darkness ensued!

But, you say, is this not atheism? Or is it not Buddhism? This blank of nothingness, this total absence of a transcendent God?

It may look that way. But in the psyche of Thérèse there is one important movement which is found neither in atheism nor in Buddhism: a total and unwavering commitment to a transcendent God whom she does not see nor hear nor touch nor feel—a transcendent God who *seems* to be absent or dead. Reasons for belief had fallen away. Yet she claimed that she now made more acts of faith than at any time in her life. Now this faith (that is to say, total commitment) was all the more pure because she believed not because of what she felt, not because of cultural props, not because of beautiful symbolism, not because it felt good to believe, not because theologians proved God's existence, not because she felt the sweet and mystical sense of God's presence. She believed because she believed. She believed God for God. And this is pure faith. It was of this faith that the Johannine Jesus spoke when he gently chided Thomas: "Blessed are those who have not seen and yet believed" (John 20:29).

## III

I have spoken of presence and absence. But the goal is vision.

Deep in the heart of every man and woman lies the desire to see God. To this desire Moses gave expression when he audaciously asked to see the face of Yahweh. To this desire the psalmist gives expression when he longs for God as the hart longs for flowing streams or as the parched earth longs for water. So great is the human longing for God. And in the mystical life this longing becomes a gaping wound, a wound of love, the wound of one who loves God but cannot see Him.

To this desire St. John of the Cross gives expression when he sings in *The Spiritual Canticle:*

> Reveal Your presence and may the vision of Your beauty be my death.

Presence here means vision; and the saint is longing, longing for the vision of God. Yet he knows that he cannot see God in this life (yes, in testimony of this he quotes the words of Yahweh to Moses) and so the only way to see God is through death.

Two visions bring death he says. One is the vision of the fabulous and venomous reptile called the basilisk which, hatched by a serpent from a cock's egg, slays by its breath or look. The other is the vision of the beauty of God. And for this second vision he would undergo a thousand deaths.

Here, then, St. John of the Cross follows the theological opinion which states that no one sees God in this life. What we can have here below is a dark, dark vision of God. "For the likeness between faith and God is so close that no other difference exists than that between believing in God and seeing him."[5] That the elect see God was taught by Pope Benedict XII in the Constitution *Benedictus Deus* of 1336: "The souls of the blessed in heaven have an intuitive and direct vision of the divine essence without the intermediary of any previously known creature. The divine essence manifests itself directly and openly in perfect clarity. The souls of the blessed enjoy it continually and will enjoy it forever. Such is eternal life."[6] St. John of the Cross, no mean theologian, was undoubtedly familiar with this document.

And so the longing for the vision of God in eternity becomes a raging fire. Nothing on the face of the earth will now satisfy the mystic longing. Any sense of presence, any vision, any locution, any rapture, any mystical experience whatsoever is no more than a foretaste of the beatifying vision of God.

## IV

I hear you say: "Presence and absence! Wonderful! But are not these mystics engaged in a pious and loving ego-trip, far, far from the immense problems of our troubled century? What about nuclear war? What about pollution of the atmosphere? What about starvation and oppression and torture?"

Let me explain. Every step of the way, the mystics are close not only to God but to the whole human family. Even (indeed especially) in those dark nights of seeming despair when God seems absent and hell lies open—even then they are very, very close to us.

For the fact is that our modern world is in a dark night. And the evils of hunger and war and oppressions are symptoms of an even deeper evil: rejection of God and deliberate choice of darkness. Many, many people are without faith, without hope, without love, lost in a morass of despair, wandering in the night, lost in this world—and who knows if they will be lost in another?

And in their dark nights the mystics go through hell, not for themselves but for the world. They taste the very despair their contemporaries taste; they resonate with the agony of those who believe that God is really dead. They are like Jesus in Geth-semani; they cry out: "Lama sabacthani!" And their unwavering faith is a light to a faithless world.

To us their lives may look irrelevant. They themselves may feel totally irrelevant—that is part of their darkness. But they are at the center of the titanic struggle for the salvation of the world. They are a beacon to all of us. Through them we are saved.

NOTES

1. *Story of a Soul,* trans. John Clarke, O.C.D. (Washington, D.C.: ICS Publications, 1975), p. 213.
2. Ibid.
3. Ibid.
4. Ibid., p. 214.
5. "The Ascent of Mount Carmel," in *The Collected Works of St. John of the Cross,* trans. Kieran Kavanaugh and Otilio Rodriguez (Washington, D.C.: ICS Publications, 1979), bk. II, chap. 9, p. 213.

# 6

# Conflict (1)

I

I spoke of the desert as a place of prayer wherein one experiences the presence of God. And so it is. But paradoxically the desert is also the place of temptation wherein one meets the devil. Indeed, thousands of holy men and women, following in the footsteps of Jesus, have retired to the wilderness precisely to meet Satan and to conquer him in bloody or unbloody conflict.

On one of my trips I became acutely aware of the diabolical dimension of the great and terrible wilderness. Whereas Jerusalem is filled with places of worship, the desert south of 'En Gedi seemed not only empty but profoundly godless. From Sedom to Eilat and from Nueiba to Sharm es Sheikh I found no synagogue, no church, no mosque, no temple. Certainly the wandering Bedouin have their place of prayer; but I did not see it. Where was God? We were warned to sleep out in the open away from rocks or clumps of grass where poisonous snakes and venomous scorpions lurked threateningly. Where was God? It is not surprising, I reflected, that holy people overcome with hunger and thirst, exhausted and weakened by the merciless heat and the piercing cold should find themselves face to face with Satan.

For when one enters the desert (whether real or metaphorical) without books and magazines, without radio and television, when one's senses are no longer bombarded by all the junk to which we are ordinarily exposed, when the top layers of our psyche are swept clean and bare and empty—then the deeper layers of the psyche rise to the surface. The inner demons lift up their ugly faces. The snakes and scorpions which were dormant or hard at work in the unconscious now raise their venomous heads and slither into the conscious mind. And we are face to face with the devil.

## II

I said that holy men and women went into the desert precisely to meet Satan.

"How terrible!" you say. "How morbid! Why should anyone want to meet Satan? Surely we should spend our lives avoiding him."

One moment. The desert fathers claimed that it was much better to meet the devil than not to meet the devil. For he is always at work; and *he is never more dangerous than when he conceals himself.* So bring him out of the darkness into the light. Face him squarely and, trusting in God, you will conquer, "for he who is in you is greater than he who is in the world" (1 John 4:4).

Besides, there is an inevitability about temptation and darkness and conflict. All this is a necessary and valuable part of human life. "No temptation: no salvation," said the fathers. Temptation is a glorious time of opportunity. When you limp away like Jacob, realizing your own brokenness and failure, crying out: "Lord, be merciful to me a sinner!"; when you throw yourself on God's mercy knowing that you yourself are a powerless, burnt-out case—then your salvation is at hand.

And there is the additional fact that unless you conquer Satan in the desert you cannot safely go into the field of action. Only when he had won the battle in the desert did Jesus embark upon his public ministry. Only after spending the night in prayer on the mountain did he choose his disciples. Only after the agony in Gethsemane did he face his passion with tranquility and courage. And many of his followers have had a similar experience. Their desert victory was the very condition of their action. Yes, while retreat to the desert may look like an escape, it is in fact a facing up to the real problems of life: it is a necessary prelude to Christian action.

And this traditional doctrine fits harmoniously with much modern psychology. Just as the desert fathers said it was good to face the devil, so wise old Jung insists that it is good and salutary—even necessary for growth—to face one's shadow and to confront one's inner demons. For we all have our shadow and our demons. No one is exempt. And the Pharisee who said he was not like the rest of men was very, very wrong. Who is without his or her fears, neuroses, anxieties? Who is untouched by those demons called the seven deadly sins: pride, covetousness, lust, gluttony, envy, anger, and sloth? Alas, alas, for the darkness in all of us!

And as long as they lurk in the unconscious, these fears, anxieties, angers, and lusts can tyrannize us—they can be compulsive, they can create havoc of all kinds. That is why any self-respecting psychologist will say: "Don't avoid them! Go through them! Bring them into the light and face them fairly and squarely. Only then will you be able to handle them."

More easily said than done. Fearing the darkness, we flee from our unconscious. Is it not more pleasant to play tennis or drink beer or watch television? But we cannot run away forever. Sooner or later the circumstances of life or a divine call or both will force us to face our unconscious. And when we do so with fortitude and courage, lo and behold, we discover that the unconscious is our friend. Yes, even the shadow can be our friend, leading us to the center of our soul where God lives in light inaccessible.

### III

I said that we are confronted with grimacing monsters of anxiety or fear or gluttony or lust or whatever. Let me here select for consideration one of these monsters which is particularly active in our day: the demon of anger leading to hatred and violence.

Psychologists give us lots of good advice about how to handle our anger, hostility, aggression. Generally, they will say that we should recognize our feelings, get in touch with them and accept them. Only in this way can we lead a rich emotional life.

When anger arises in the heart from the frustration of not getting what we want, then the worst possible thing is to deny it, repress it, pretend it is not there. "I'm not angry. Ha! Ha!" For this is to ram it into the unconscious where it will fester, causing acute depression or exploding in some unforeseen way. Much better, then, to recognize it and tell your friends about it. In short, learn to live with your shadowy demon and to accept him or her.

Now all this makes sense. And I have often told people to sit with their anger. Sit in the lotus! Get in touch with it! Accept it!

Having said this, however, it is also true that this is psychology for a bourgeois society. Talk to someone born in Belfast or Beirut or Johannesburg. Talk to someone who has seen his or her father humiliated by the police in the early hours of the morning. Talk to someone who has been imprisoned for a crime he or she did not commit. Talk to people who have suffered crushing injustice and tell me what they say. You will see that real anger cannot be handled by psychology alone, but only through profound healing, authentic conversion, mystical transformation.

Paul was well aware of this. I do not say that his problem was anger, but it was some kindred emotion; and Paul laments: "For I do not do what I want, but I do the very thing I hate. . . . So then it is no longer I that do it, but sin which dwells within me" (Romans 7:15, 17). What a struggle went on in the breast of Paul! And he was acutely aware of his need for a savior. "Wretched man that I am! Who will deliver me from this body of death? Thanks be to God through Jesus Christ our Lord" (Romans 7:25).

Paul is aware of two laws: the law of God in his inmost self and another law in his members. But, thanks to the grace of Jesus, it is the law of God that triumphs. "For the law of the Spirit of life in Christ Jesus has set me free from the law of sin and death" (Romans 8:2).

If, then, you would follow Paul, and if you feel drawn to contemplation, I would urge you to sit quietly in the presence of God and in the cloud of unknowing. Get in touch with your anger. Let it surface, while you remain with your deep, true self where you meet God. The storm may be terrible; you may find it intolerable to sit; all hell may break loose inside you. But remain with it; don't give up; and finally you will cry trimphantly with Paul: "The law of the Spirit of life in Christ Jesus has set me free from the law of sin and death" (Romans 8:2).

In this process, the first step is acceptance, integration, interior peace and calm. This solves the problem of fragmentation and inner division. But it is not enough. Terrorist and establishment alike have integrated anger, only to direct it with cold-blooded hatred to destructive ends. Much more is asked of the Christian. He or she must go beyond inner peace to an interiorization of the Sermon on the Mount: "But I say to you that hear, love your enemies, do good to those who hate you . . ."

(Luke 6:27). He or she must come to see the working of God even in the quagmire of injustice. And no psychology will help us do that but only the love of God in Christ Jesus our Lord. Only through profound conversion of heart, the gift of the Spirit, only through mystical transformation do we come to live the Gospel existentially.

Now the Gospel does not tell us to annihilate our anger (Jesus did not annihilate his) nor does it tell us to ram it into the unconscious. Rather must we transform it (or, more correctly, let God transform it) into a seeking of the kingdom of God and His justice. And, when this is done, destructive anger becomes just anger. It becomes the anger of a Mahatma Gandhi, a Martin Luther King, a Dorothy Day, a Thomas Merton, a Lech Walesa. Now it is the just anger of people who have harnessed all their energies in the service of the oppressed. In them *the demon of anger has become a friend.* Overpowering and uncontrollable anger has become an enlightened passion for justice. But this has only happened (let me repeat it) through a profound conversion of heart which is nothing less than mystical. "Thanks be to God through Jesus Christ our Lord!"

And what I say of anger is equally true of the other deadly sins. They can be transformed into their opposites. The demons become our friends.

## IV

But let me return to the children of Israel.

Their wandering in the desert was filled with temptation. And Paul sternly warns the Corinthians not to be like them since "God was not pleased; for they were overthrown in the wilderness" (1 Corinthians 10:5). But why was God not pleased? What was their sin?

At first one might say that their main sin was that they grumbled and complained. The desert was too much for them and they longed for the fleshpots of Egypt—the fish, the cucumbers, the leeks, the onions, and the garlic:

> Would that we had died in the land of Egypt! Or would that we had died in the wilderness! Why does the Lord bring us into the land, to fall by the sword? Our wives and our little ones will become a prey; would it not be better for us to go back to Egypt? [Numbers 14:2–3]

They indeed grumbled. But the grumbling and discontent led to a more serious sin: doubt, lack of faith. They doubted Moses; they doubted themselves; they doubted their call. And finally, when Moses climbed the mountain, they doubted God and persuaded Aaron to make a golden calf. That is why they were destroyed by serpents and twenty-three thousand fell in a single day.

Their grumbling was an expression of what we now call *anxiety*. They were anxious about their future, about their wives and little ones. And anxiety led them to turn away from God.

We know that the demon of anxiety is one of the most insidious monsters in the modern psyche. Apart from conscious anxiety about yesterday and tomorrow, there is that unconscious anxiety which can become compulsive, driving people to alcohol, to drugs, to inordinate sex, to compulsive craving for power, and even to self-destruction. It can drive people to manipulate and exploit others, not from hatred, but from a desire to prove themselves and to allay their inner fears. And it can drive out faith. Consumed by anxiety, we cannot believe that God loves and protects us; we act as though all depended upon ourselves; we are practical atheists. Hence the Gospel constantly attributes anxiety to lack of faith: "Why are you anxious . . . O men of little faith?" (Matthew 6:28).

You ask: "Must we cast out this demon? Or can he or she also become a friend?"

Psychologists tell us that anxiety is an inescapable part of human living and that it will be with us to the end. Nevertheless, I believe that this demon is gradually transformed through persevering contemplative prayer. When we learn *to sit with our anxiety*, agonizing though this may be; when we allow it to come to the surface of consciousness; when we learn to get in touch with it and accept it; when we get in touch with the deeper law of the Spirit of Life in Christ Jesus—then our salvation will come through the gift of profound conversion of heart.

For contemplative prayer brings an ongoing liberation. As destructive anger becomes just anger, so destructive anxiety becomes compassionate concern for ourselves and for others. This is the concern of the good angels (if I may borrow from St. Francis de Sales), who watch over us with tender care but never lose their peace. Once again, a demon has become a friend.

## V

The mystical life can be described as a journey into the depths of one's being, a journey to the true self and through the true self to God, Who is the center. Down, down I go through alternate layers of light and darkness, meeting all the slimy monsters and frightening demons that inhabit the subliminal world. And if I progress far enough, I meet not only my own little monsters: I meet the monsters of the human race. I meet the root causes of war, oppression, torture, hunger, terrorism. I meet hatred, despair, injustice, atheism, darkness, I meet archetypal evil. And, horror of horrors, I meet it in myself.

"In myself?" you say. "How can that be? How can the evils of the world be in poor little me? How can I be responsible for massacres of innocent people, for torture, for oppression of the poor?"

Alas, we are all responsible. For we all share in the collective unconscious of the human family. We are not isolated monads but members of a species, members of a living and conscious body.

Most of us are not in touch with this collective unconscious. We are far too superficial for that. So, when things go wrong, we point an accusing finger at princes and politicians or at terrorists and revolutionaries. But mystics who enter deeply into the inner desert meet archetypal evil and, with God's grace, they conquer it. Some then enter the world of politics or economics or law or whatever—and their influence is crucial. Others help the destitute poor or the underprivileged or the handicapped. Others feel that their vocation is just to pray and suffer for the salvation of the world. But whatever they do, they are the true social workers and they change our world.

# 7

# Conflict (2)

I

The synoptic gospels tell us that Jesus was led by the Spirit into the wilderness to be tempted by the devil. For forty days and forty nights he fasted and then, when he was hungry, he came face to face with evil.

Victorious, Jesus returns in the power of the Spirit to the world of people and to his public ministry. So great is his power that the people exclaim: "With authority he commands even the unclean spirits, and they obey him" (Mark 1:27). And at the end of his life Jesus can say confidently: "Now shall the ruler of the world be cast out" (John 12:31). And of Satan he can say clearly: "He has no power over me" (John 14:30).

Yet temptation was woven into the very texture of Jesus' life. St. Luke tells us that the evil one "departed from him until an opportune time" (Luke 4:13), as if to say that Satan was constantly looking for opportunities to overthrow him. And Jesus was often troubled in spirit with a trouble that reached a great climax in Gethsemane.

The temptations of Jesus, however, were different from those I outlined in the last chapters. Whereas our temptations come mainly (but not exclusively) from inner demons, the offspring of original sin, Jesus had no original sin. He met objective evil. He met the implacable enemy of human nature who can never become our friend because he is irrevocably committed to destruction.

II

In order to understand the traditional doctrine of temptation it is necessary to say a word about the mystical understanding of the human psyche.

The old authors based their psychology on Plato and Aristotle, making necessary additions and modifications. One such addition was their doctrine of the apex or center of the soul—the citadel of the soul, the deepest part of the human person, the place where the human meets the divine. This was the mysterious area of primordial commitment, the sovereign point of the spirit which can be touched only by God. Hidden and secret, it was concealed even from Satan who could not enter *unless invited to do so by a pact whereby one committed oneself totally to evil.*

Today we grasp at some similar center when we speak of the mystery of the human person or of the true self or of identity, or when we talk about the fundamental option. We say that this deep self is only discovered gradually. Frequently it is uncovered through the suffering of analysis which brings joy, because I am liberated from the superego, and pain, because I discover not who I was told to be, not what the law commands me to be, but who I really am. Again, the paths of mysticism and psychoanalysis cross! But let me return to mystical psychology.

The psyche is divided into sense and spirit. Ordinarily Satan (who cannot get to the center without a clear invitation) takes his stand at the gateway between sense and spirit. He may have stood here when he invited Jesus to turn the stones into bread.

But besides sense and the deep, deep center, there is an in-between area of spirit to which the evil one has access. St. John of the Cross speaks of shattering encounters with evil which proceed "nakedly from spirit to spirit"; and he says that "the horror the evil spirit causes . . . if he reaches the spiritual part is unbearable."[1] So violent is this encounter that the person would die if it lasted for long:

> This consternation is greater suffering than any other torment in this life. Since this horrendous communication proceeds from spirit to spirit manifestly and somewhat incorporeally, it in a way transcends all sensory pain. This spiritual suffering does not last long, for if it did, the soul would depart from the body due to this violent communication.[2]

Only enlightened mystics who have reached a high degree of spiritual maturity are capable of encountering evil in this frightening way.

Let me here pause to add that as one can horrendously meet evil at this deep and spiritual level, so one can joyfully meet good at the same level—and this is a powerful enlightenment. *Spirit meets spirit.* Surely there was something of this in the encounter of Mary and Elizabeth when both were filled with the Holy Spirit and Mary raised her voice to cry: "*Magnificat!*" Surely there was something of this at the meeting of Magdalen with Jesus when he said: "Mary" and she exclaimed: "Rabboni." Here is the great mysticism of interpersonal encounter. But let me return to Jesus and the evil one.

One of his temptations takes the form of a mystical experience—though not of a horrendous and frightening nature. Luke tells us that "the devil took him up and showed him all the kingdoms of the world in a moment of time" (Luke 4:5). This must have been a flash of light akin to that which some people have at the time of death when they momentarily see their whole lives in a panoramic vision. In the same way Jesus, in a split second, sees all the kingdoms of the world. What a mystical experience!

And for the Christian who believes that Jesus was the Incarnate Word it is indeed mind-boggling to reflect that *he was so human as to undergo a mystical experience under the influence of Satan.* Yet Luke says just that.

And St. John of the Cross talks constantly about diabolical interference in the mystical life. So much so, that he is extremely wary of all kinds of enlightenments, raptures, voices, visions, ecstasies, and the like. Assuredly the evil one can do no harm to one who, unmasking him as did Jesus, turns to God. But one who accepts such mystical experiences and acts on them is a pitifully deceived false mystic.

Surely there is here a vital lesson for contemporary men and women. So many seekers, dabbling in Asian mysticism or in drugs or in the occult, have big enlightenments and beautiful illuminations. And they like to tell their friends or to contribute articles to magazines. Let them reflect carefully that Jesus had a big illumination caused by Satan. Let them reflect that the mystical path is full of danger and that discernment is of cardinal importance.

## III

The direction of the temptation is even more stunning. Satan promises Jesus authority over the whole world on one condition:

If you, then, will worship me, it shall be yours. [Luke 4:7]

Is it possible that the Son of God should be invited to worship evil? Is it possible that the all-holy one should be tempted to make a total commitment to evil? Luke seems to say precisely this.

And if Jesus is asked to make a total commitment to evil, can we doubt that the same temptation has come to his followers through the ages? At the very peak-point of the mystical life, when they were in touch with their true selves and the deepest level of spirit, they have been tempted to choose evil. The desert fathers say grimly that the devils rejoice more in the fall of such a sublime mystic than in the destruction of thousands of lesser lights.

St. Ignatius points to this in his *Spiritual Exercises* when he asks the retreatant to reflect on the sin of the angels and on the sin of Adam. According to the theology of his time, these were sins not of human weakness but of deliberate choice—a choice made in total liberty and without pressure from the passions.

Let me pause again to observe that we here find one of the unique characteristics of Judeo-Christian mysticism. At the very peak-point of the mystical life, when one is in touch with the true self, one is still capable of evil and, indeed, of the greatest evil. I see nothing quite like this in Hinduism or in Buddhism.

And if consummate mystics have been tempted to make a total commitment to evil, how much more the small fry! Indeed, this is the only real temptation in human life and to yield to it is the only real sin. Isolated acts of pride, covetousness, lust, gluttony, envy, anger, and sloth—these are not tragedies. They are part of human living. Christian tradition has consistently taught that no one is free from original sin; and if one promptly rises from the mire, isolated sins can be a distinct advantage on the path to God. The real tragedy is when people are drawn to change their direction, to commit themselves to evil, to change their very identity (for our identity is constituted by that to which we are committed) and to surrender the very apex of their soul to evil. This is the ultimate temptation; this is to choose hell.

Let me put it in another way. As faith is commitment to God, so sin in its radical form is commitment to evil. All lesser temptations are dangerous only in so far as they lead to this. Concretely, this definitive sin could take the form of a total commitment to any of the seven deadly sins. And this finally is a commitment to the definitive destruction of oneself and others. Just as the first commandment is to love God, oneself and one's neighbor, so the final sin is to commit oneself to hate God, to hate self, and to hate one's neighbor.

"Hate God?" you say. "Why should anyone hate God?"

It sounds strange, but deep in the human heart is a tendency to forget God, to hate God, to reject God, to put oneself in God's place. *Non serviam!* "I will not serve!" The old authors called it pride and, alas, it is very much alive today. Moreover, the person who hates God hates self and the whole universe—for God is not separate from His world.

Yes, the fact is that the great struggle in human life is for the apex or citadel of the soul, the deep, deep center where we make our fundamental option and our ultimate commitment either to good or to evil. When a person committed to evil changes this commitment and with it his or her horizon, this is called conversion. When a person committed to good turns toward evil, this is called sin.

Again you ask: "Why do we sin? Why do we blind ourselves to the true light? How is it possible for the human person deliberately to choose evil? How come evil even exists—if it does exist?"

These are questions which have baffled theologians since Augustine and before. They speak of the mystery of iniquity: *mysterium iniquitatis*. And it is indeed a sobering mystery.

IV

I spoke of how consummate mystics can be invited to choose evil. Ordinarily, however, temptation is a long process and the aim of the tempter is to deceive and draw us along the path to evil. Remember how Paul tells the Corinthians that Satan disguises himself as an angel of light, and he writes:

> But I am afraid that as the serpent deceived Eve by his cunning, your thoughts will be led astray from a sincere and pure devotion to Christ. [2 Corinthians 11:3]

The serpent! Temptation is primarily deceit by a crafty enemy. And how deceitful evil can be! One of the most subtle temptations of Jesus comes from his best friend. Remember how Peter, dismayed at the thought of the passion and death of Jesus, exclaims: "God forbid, Lord! This shall never happen to you" (Matthew 16:22); and Jesus with unwonted severity confronts him: "Get behind me, Satan! You are a hindrance to me; for you are not on the side of God, but of men" (Matthew 16:23). Unwittingly, and under the guise of compassion, Peter was doing the work of Satan, trying to deflect Jesus from his sublime vocation to suffer and die.

No spiritual writer has unmasked the process of deception with more psychological insight than St. Ignatius. He would have us constantly reflect on the inner movements, examine our consciousness and detect not only any movement towards sin but also the movements which lead to anxiety, fear, commotion, loss of peace. For in one who would travel the path to God, as the great goods are peace and joy and the other fruits of the spirit, so the greatest evils after sin are turmoil and anxiety leading to loss of faith, loss of hope, loss of charity, and change of commitment.

When it comes to outlining the actual process, St. Ignatius is clear. The path of Satan is one of riches, honor, pride, leading to all other evils. The path of Jesus, on the other hand, is one of poverty, insults, humility, leading to all good.

But even as I write, I hear your exasperated voice: "Your whole thesis is individualistic and self-centered. What has it to do with the world torn asunder with social problems? Surely the great sins of today are the sins of nations, not those of individuals."

I agree. But my thesis is not individualistic. While it is true that the center of the soul is intensely personal and that sin is finally a personal choice, still the paths of Ignatius are eminently relevant not only for individuals but also for societies. Let me explain.

We know that the great problem of today is nuclear war. We also know that if there is a nuclear war (which God forbid) it will be fought *for money, for oil, for petrodollars.* For it is no secret that when, in a given society, a significant number of people are totally committed to economic progress, when they are willing to sell arms to all and sundry for money, when they are then committed to their own and their country's affluence and prestige—then they forget God or put themselves in the place of God. And from this stems all evil, including nuclear war. This is the inexorable path described by Ignatius.

We also know that if a significant number of people are willing to renounce affluence, if they care little about prestige and all about justice, if they empty themselves in a *kenosis* like Jesus —then they can save the world. And this again is the Ignatian path.

Commitment to a poverty that leads to kenosis, far from being individualistic, is the greatest service one can render to today's world.

### V

All this may sound somber. Indeed the stakes are high. Yet the New Testament is vibrantly optimistic: "Be of good cheer. I have overcome the world" (John 16:33). The wounded stag appears on the hill and by his wounds we are healed and saved. Through his blood we triumph in every temptation. Anyone who calls on the name of Jesus will be victorious "because if you confess with your lips that Jesus is Lord and believe in your heart that God raised him from the dead, you will be saved" (Romans 10:9). Hence the words which bring salvation are: "Jesus is Lord."

Finally, let me cite an ancient and new Catholic belief that we are always safe in the company of the Virgin Mary. Tradition tells us that the demons fly from her in horror lest they be crushed by the heel which pressed upon the serpent's head. When the children of Israel carried the ark of the covenant into battle they were always victorious. And Mary is the ark of the covenant in the New Dispensation.

## NOTES

1. "The Dark Night," in *The Collected Works of St. John of the Cross,* trans. Kieran Kavanaugh and Otilio Rodriguez (Washington, D.C.: ICS Publications, 1979), bk. II, chap. 23, 1.5.
2. Ibid., 1.9.

# 8

# Covenant and Conversion

I

Following the cloud by day and the pillar of fire by night, Moses and the people travelled through the great and terrible wilderness to Mount Sinai—to Horeb, to the mountain of God. And our little band of scholars, following in their footsteps, came to the holy mountain.

We climbed Gebel Musa and enjoyed the breathtaking view from its ethereal summit. Whether or not Moses climbed this mountain nobody knows. An ancient tradition claims that the nearby Gebel Serba is the genuine article. Be that as it may, our journey was no less politically tense than that of Moses and his people. The Israelis were withdrawing by stages from Sinai in accordance with the agreement of Camp David, and we passed checkpoint after checkpoint as we crossed that desolate border into Egypt.

At the foot of the mountain stands the ancient monastery of St. Catherine. Founded as a shrine by Empress Helena in 327, becoming a combination of monastery and fortress in 530, it is one of the oldest continuously occupied buildings in the whole world. But the monks value their obscurity and we had little chance to talk with them. Further down is the great, broad plain where the children of Israel supposedly camped and watched their great leader wend his lonely way up the mountain to meet God in a thick cloud amidst peals of thunder and flashes of lightning.

## II

With the covenant we are at the heart of Judeo-Christian religious experience. Moses is the mediator of this covenant as Jesus will be the mediator of a new covenant. In both cases the binding force is love. God has loved His people. He has led them out of Egypt. He has carried them on eagles' wings and brought them to Himself. His love has been steadfast and unfailing. And in return the people are summoned to an unrestricted, unconditional love. The powerful words of Deuteronomy echo through the centuries and continue to ring vibrantly in the ears of contemporary men and women:

> Hear, O Israel; the Lord our God is one Lord; and you shall love the Lord your God with all your heart, and with all your soul, and with all your might. [Deuteronomy 6:4,5]

Here God asks for a total love, an unrestricted love, a love that goes on and on and on, a love that cannot not lead to altered states of consciousness, to inner revolution, to the most profound mystical experience. When we are faithful to the covenant, when we receive God's love and respond with all our heart and with all our soul and with all our might, then we undergo *metanoia* or conversion or change of heart. This is the transformation, the revolution in consciousness, the death and resurrection which is at the very heart of the Christian mystical life. It is an experience which is at once personal and communal. Moses entered the cloud alone but the people shared his experience when they cried: "All that the Lord has spoken we will do" (Exodus 19:8). In Paul's enigmatic phrase, "they were baptized into Moses in the cloud and in the sea" (1 Corinthians 10:2).

### III

The covenant, far from being a superhuman call, is a way of becoming fully alive, a way of becoming fully human. And likewise metanoia, even in its deepest and most mystical form, is a completely human experience. In fact the way to metanoia can be described in terms of fidelity to the transcendental precepts which reflect the basic dynamism of the human Spirit: *Be attentive, be intelligent, be reasonable, be responsible, be in love.* As is clear, the covenant is concerned with the last of these: *Be in love.* But (and this is important) a close look at the covenant reveals an even more fundamental and challenging transcendental precept:

> Accept love
> or
> Be loved
> or
> Let yourself be loved

This precept is basic to Exodus and Deuteronomy and the Psalms, where we hear constantly of the great things God has done for His people, of the great love He has manifested for them. It stands out beautifully in Deutero-Isaiah where Yahweh tells His people: "You are precious in my eyes and honored, and I love you" (Isaiah 43:4). It is the message of the First Epistle of St. John: "In this is love, not that we loved God but that he loved us . . ." (1 John 4:10). And the same epistle says: "We love because he first loved us" (1 John 4:19).

From this it becomes clear that the great challenge of the

Christian life is to receive love, to open our hearts to the one who knocks, to accept him into the very depths of our being.

Nor is this easy. We all know that human nature is perversely full of paradox. On the one hand we long for love. The deepest longing of the human heart is for love—for human love and divine love. On the other hand we fight against the very love we long for; we shut it out; we slam the door so that even God cannot enter.

And so we poor humans must learn to be loved. One way of doing this is through meditation on the Scriptures. We can take a phrase like "We love because he first loved us" or "You are precious in my eyes. . . . I love you." We can take one such phrase and turn it over and over in our mind and heart. We relish it. We savor it. We let it talk to us. *We live it*. And one day we shout out: "We love because He first loved us! Now I see. Now I understand. I never realized this until now. *Eureka!* I am loved. I am precious in His eyes and He loves me."

Or another way is simply to ask God to love us: "Give me your love and your grace, for this is enough for me."

Or again we may learn to open our hearts to human love. For never let us forget that authentic human love is God's love made incarnate. So accept the love which comes your way. If you think that nobody loves you, this is probably because you are unconsciously warding off love. You just are not taking it in. Accept it with gratitude and you will experience joy.

To accept love, then, is the first step in fulfilling the covenant; it is the first step towards metanoia.

## IV

And now I hear you say: "But why is human nature so perverse? Why do we refuse love? Why do we shut out the very thing we want? How explain this?"

Fallen nature is full of mystery and contradiction. Alas, deep down in all of us is a tendency to hate ourselves and to destroy ourselves. Sometimes this stems from an unconscious sense of guilt, unconscious desire for self-punishment and self-flagellation. Whatever the cause, some people have an acute sense of their own radical unlovableness. They have the "I'm not OK" syndrome. They feel deeply, "It just isn't possible that anyone, including God, could possibly love me." And this paralyzes them, making them reject love. Such people must learn to love themselves; and one way to do this is to accept the love of God and the love of people in the way I have just described.

Besides, in all of us there is a fear of intimacy and a fear of love. You see, just as human love unites us with a human person, so divine love unites us with God and with the universe and with everyone—it unites us with the totality. And something inside us fights against this. "I want my independence. I want to build my own kingdom. I will not serve. I will not submit to love." This is the deadly sin of pride which strikes roots in all of us.

And there is one more point. Receiving love seems wonderfully consoling. What greater joy than to accept the immense love of God?

Yes and no. St. John of the Cross tells us that as we come close to God we discover that He is like night to the soul. The love of God is very different from any other love we know or experience. It is so unfamiliar, so strange, so powerful, so unconditional that it blinds our faculties and plunges us into painful darkness. Sometimes God's love is like nothingness, emptiness, blackness. Small wonder that we fly in panic from the hound of heaven.

Yes, love blinds us, consumes us, devours us. But the pain is accompanied by joy. And as we learn to become like little children, as we learn to empty ourselves, as we learn to open the door and keep it open so that God and people can enter, then we come to experience that we are loved and that we are lovable. We are lovable because we were created in the image of God; we are lovable because we were redeemed by Jesus Christ. Redemption has made us lovable, even more lovable than if we had never sinned.

Such is the theory. It is through meditation and, above all, through covenant mysticism that this theory becomes life. Through deep meditation we discover the true self and, entering into a new state of consciousness, we realize existentially with great joy that we are indeed loved.

### V

Accepting love, we return it not only to God but to people—to everyone we meet without exception. "If God so loved us, we also ought to love one another . . ." (1 John 4:11). There seems to be a psychological law that authentic love cannot remain locked up within the human heart. It rebounds to the one who loves us. And if this lover identifies with all men and women (as does Jesus) then his love ricochets from us to all men and women. If this lover identifies in a special way with the poor and the suffering and the oppressed (as does Jesus) then his love ricochets from us to the poor and the suffering and the oppressed.

Indeed, the covenantal love found in metanoia penetrates all human relationships—love of husband and wife, love of parents and children, love between friends, love in community, love for the church, love for country, love for the world. All these loves are caught up in the mystical love of the covenant. They share in the Christian mystical experience.

### VI

Most of what I have said about metanoia and covenant love applies equally to the old and the new covenant. Now let me say a word about the metanoia which is specifically Christian.

The New Testament constantly refers back to Deuteronomy telling us that the first commandment is to love God with our whole heart and soul and mind and strength. And at the Last Supper, as the new Moses, Jesus mediates another commandment in his own blood. As Moses had sprinkled the blood of animals on the altar and on the people, thus uniting God and humanity, so Jesus will shed his own blood, reconciling the human family with God our Father. "Drink of it all of you; for this is my blood of the covenant, which is poured out for many for the forgiveness of sins" (Matthew 26:28).

This new covenant is renewed in the Eucharist when we gather to break bread and to celebrate the great event that has saved us:

> Christ has died
> Christ has risen
> Christ will come again.

It is not surprising, then, that from the earliest times the Eucharist, the new covenant in his blood, has been the principal source of Christian religious experience and of Christian mystical experience. Participating in this sacrament we receive the love of Jesus into the depths of our being; we eat his body and drink his blood; united with him we offer ourselves to the Father: "Abba, Father!"

Such is the new covenant. Now let me point to the principal characteristics of the metanoia it engenders.

First, it is a change of heart whereby we commit ourselves totally to Jesus, the Risen Lord. Now we realize that he loves us immensely for the wounded stag has appeared on the hill. And filled with love and wounded with love we cry out with Paul: "What shall I do, Lord" (Acts of Apostles 20:10). Jesus, in turn, leads us to the Father. Remember how he prayed to his Father "that the love with which thou hast loved me may be in them, and I in them" (John 17:26). This means that the Spirit is in us and Jesus is in us. And so, one with Jesus and filled with the Spirit, we cry out: "Abba, Father!"

Second, Christian metanoia is a change of heart whereby we commit ourselves totally to the gospel. "Repent, and believe in the gospel" (Mark 1:15). This does not mean that we make a commitment to scriptural exegesis. It does not mean that we make a commitment to a mere understanding of the gospel. It means that *we make a commitment to live the gospel*—not to live it in the world of Corinth or Philippi or Rome or Alexandria, but to live it in our modern world with its turmoil and anguish, with its poverty and oppression, with its glittering scientific achievements and its dismal social failures.

Third, Christian metanoia is a change of heart whereby we commit ourselves to the community. Here the community is the church. Not the church in a narrow, sectarian sense of that word. The Council gave us a new vision of the church as the community of the disciples of Jesus united among themselves and united with Jews, Moslems, Hindus, Buddhists. This is a church which feels united with all men and women of good will, even those who are atheist or agnostic. To love the church is to love the whole world: to be committed to the church is to be committed to the world. Listen to the words of the Council:

> All men and women are called to be part of this catholic unity of the People of God, . . . And there belong to it or are related to it in various ways, the Catholic faithful as well as all who believe in Christ, and indeed the whole of human-kind. For all are called to salvation by the grace of God.[1]

To love the church is to love the whole of humankind.

### VII

In the Christian life the initial metanoia is baptism which, for Paul, is the experience of death and rebirth. "Do you not know that all of us who have been baptized into Christ Jesus were baptized into his death? We were buried therefore with him by baptism into death, so that as Christ was raised from the dead . . . we too might walk in newness of life" (Romans 6: 3, 4).

When we think of baptism we usually think of the ritual pouring of water; but Paul is talking here of the great spiritual experience underlying the pouring of water. Probably he is thinking of his own mystical experience on the road to Damascus where he died a great death and "suffered the loss of all things" (Philippians 3:8) in order to rise to newness of life. For Paul this was clearly a painful experience followed by great joy.

And the same holds true for metanoia in our lives. Ordinarily it is preceded by suffering, by shock, by pain, by death. We hit rock bottom before rising with ecstatic joy.

But baptism is no more than a beginning. Metanoia is an ongoing process extending throughout life and reaching a mighty climax in death. Paul vividly compares himself to a runner in the Isthmian games. He has not arrived at the goal; he has not yet made the grade; he is still imperfect. "Brethren, I do not consider that I have made it my own; but one thing I do, forgetting what lies behind and straining forward to what lies ahead, I press on towards the goal for the prize of the upward call of God in Christ Jesus" (Philippians 3:13,14).

The process! Like Paul we are all on the way. Like Paul we have our blind spots, our unconverted areas, our unregenerate dimension. It is indeed strange to see how people can be totally converted to the gospel in some areas and radically blind in others. How shocking to see people filled with compassion and advocating war! We raise our hands in horror but we do the same ourselves. We see the speck in the eye of others but miss the log in our own.

But as the process of accepting love and loving goes on, it brings a change of consciousness whereby the heart of stone becomes a heart of flesh. Ordinarily this is a gradual process accompanied by occasional flashes of insight, by falls and retrogression and stupidities and mistakes. The great challenge is to remain open to love, to remain open to change, to remain open to growth.

Sometimes (perhaps three or four times in a lifetime) metanoia may take the form of a great upheaval, an inner revolution, a violent shock through which one painfully yet joyfully acquires a new vision and sets out on a new path. These are times of crisis when one realizes that this life of love is an awful risk, leading us to a place we do not know by a path we know not.

## VIII

From all that has been said it will be clear that metanoia is the very core and center of Christian prayer and of Christian mysticism. Meditation which does not lead to metanoia cannot be called Christian. It may bring us to wonderful altered states of consciousness; it may leave us refreshed, rested, and relaxed; it may bring us to trance and ecstacy; it may enhance our human potential a hundredfold. But if it does not bring fidelity to the covenant of love, it cannot be called Christian. On this point St. Teresa of Avila is enlightening. She speaks of rapture and ecstasy and ligature and various states of consciousness in the lower mansions of the soul; but when she comes to the seventh and last mansion she speaks almost exclusively about love of neighbor. "Beloved, if God so loved us, we also ought to love one another" (1 John 4:11).

You say: "But what kind of metanoia is called for in our day? You have said we must live the gospel in this modern world and not in Corinth or in Philippi. What are you getting at?"

First of all, let me say that we live at a turning point in human history; we are in the throes of what Karl Jaspers called *an axial age.* We are faced with the alternatives of destroying ourselves in a nuclear holocaust or advancing to a new anthropological stage—to a new stage in evolution. In these critical circumstances, our first duty is to get in touch with the new age in which we live, to see the signs of the times, to resonate with the problems of contemporary men and women. We cannot do this without a profound conversion of heart that will take us out of one world and into another. This is the conversion, the renewal, the updating, the aggiornamento to which the Council called all Christians—and not only all Christians but all men and women. Alas, so many committed Christians continue to live in a world that no longer exists and to operate through structures that have long since died. It is this that makes them irrelevant. Let us open our hearts to the new global consciousness that is emerging everywhere. Let us read the gospel in our new historical setting. If we do so, we will find that this gospel takes on a new splendor and a new meaning—a wealth of meaning that the biblical authors themselves could not have foreseen. And if we strive to be faithful to the covenant we will likewise discover that the covenant takes on a new and startling meaning in this new world which is painfully coming to birth.

And in this basic conversion to the modern world we will find ample guidance in the Second Vatican Council, in numerous statements of the World Council of Churches, in those prophetic voices that are raised in different continents throughout the world. These summon us to a change of heart and a revolution in consciousness without which the human family may well perish. About this inner revolution I will speak more in detail as this book develops. Here let me mention certain specific areas where the covenant takes on new and lustrous meaning in a new world.

1) Fidelity to the covenant in our world will bring a conversion to peace. If we have experienced God's love for us and if this has led us to love the world, we cannot but recoil from the prospect of war and long for peace. We will recoil not only from war but from any kind of violence whether it be the institutionalized violence of established governments or the revolutionary violence of terrorists. Moreover, conversion of heart will enable us to pay the price, to make the sacrifices which peace demands —if necessary to change our life-style, to cut down on luxuries, to share with others. If we really want peace we may have to die and to suffer the loss of all things as did Paul on the road to Damascus. "Blessed are the peacemakers . . ." takes on a new splendor in our day.

2) Fidelity to the covenant will bring a conversion to the poor. If we have experienced God's love for us and if we want to respond according to the spirit of the gospel, we will love in a special way the poor, the afflicted, the exploited, the underprivileged, the hungry. But (and again this is the crux) conversion of heart alone will enable us to pay the price and to make the sacrifices—to lower our standard of living, to share with the poor, to fight against a system which exploits and terrorizes and oppresses the third world. If we want to love the poor we may have to suffer the loss of everything as did Paul. "Blessed are the poor . . ." takes on a new splendor in our day.

3) Fidelity to the covenant will bring a conversion to those who do not share our religious convictions. It will lead us to love not only Christians of various denominations but also Jews, Moslems, Hindus, Buddhists. Thoroughgoing conversion alone will enable us to rise above the narrow sectarianism which has

caused horrible wars and continues to divide our contemporary world.

4) Fidelity to the covenant will bring conversion to woman and to those feminine values without which we cannot build a just and peaceful society. For Christians, I myself associate this with a conversion to the Virgin Mary and a renewed realization of her role in the mystical life.

5) Fidelity to the covenant will bring conversion to our contemporary world. Let us now listen to prophetic voices wherever they are. Let us repent of our failure to appreciate the scientific achievements and the prophetic insights of so many thinkers who built our modern world.

### IX

I have spoken of our need for conversion. Now let me quote two prophets of our century. The first is a scientist. Here are the words of Albert Einstein:

> We must never relax our efforts to arouse in the people of the world, and especially in governments, an awareness of the unprecedented disaster which they are absolutely certain to bring upon themselves unless there is a fundamental change in their attitude towards one another as well as in their concept of the future. The unleashed power of the atom has changed everything except our way of thinking.

To change our way of thinking and to change our hearts. This is the challenge.

My second prophet is a religious leader. Pope Paul, addressing the General Assembly of the United Nations in 1965, spoke as follows:

> The hour has struck for our *conversion*, for personal transformation, for interior renewal. We must get used to thinking of man in a new way; and in a new way of man's life in com-

mon; with a new manner too of conceiving the paths of history and the destiny of the world, according to the words of St. Paul: "You must be clothed in the new self, which is created in God's image, justified and sanctified through the truth" (Ephesians 4:23). The hour has struck for a halt, a moment of recollection, of reflection, almost of prayer. A moment to think anew of our common origin, our history, our common destiny. Today as never before, in our era so marked by human progress, there is need for an appeal to the moral conscience of man.

The hour has indeed struck for a change of heart, for a revolution in consciousness, for a renewed and mystical conversion to the covenant.

### NOTE

1. *Lumen Gentium* C.2, 13; *The Documents of Vatican II*, ed. Walter M. Abbot (New York: American Press, 1966), p. 32.

# 9

# Jesus
# Mysticism

I

I started this book with a search for the unique dimension of Christian mysticism. Having spent many years in a comparative study of Buddhism and Christianity, I wanted to see what was special and unique about the mystical experience of Christians. And I found something very distinctive in the sense of presence, the felt sense of presence of a loving and transcendent God whom I call Father. This is a God Who is not only transcendent but also immanent because He dwells in the depths of my being.

However, the sense of a transcendent God is not uniquely Christian. While in Jerusalem I had the privilege and the joy of praying side by side with Jews at the Western Wall of the Temple. And as we swayed to and fro, calling on God and reciting the psalms, I became acutely aware of my kinship with Jews and our sense of a common Father. Again, in Cairo I prayed in mosques, touching the ground with my forehead, and again I realized that Moslems have a profound and reverent sense of God's transcendent presence. Yes, Jews, Moslems, Christians, we acknowledge the same God; we sense the same loving prsence; we are all children of Abraham.

What is uniquely Christian, then, is not the sense of God's presence but involvement with Jesus Christ, the Risen Lord. The fervent Christian is led into a mystical relationship with Jesus, a relationship which, beginning with presence, leads to union and on to identification. And then, one with Jesus in the Spirit, he or she cries out: "Abba, Father!"

Let me now say something about this mystical relationship with Jesus.

II

This mystical relationship with Jesus is, of course, based on the New Covenant in his blood. The starting point is his love for me—"he loved me and gave himself for me"(Galatians 2:20). He is the good shepherd who lays down his life for his sheep; he is the servant of Yahweh who was wounded for our sins and bruised for our iniquity; he is the wounded stag who is wounded because we are wounded. A deep realization of his love leads to a sense of presence, *an obscure yet tangible sense of presence. And this in turn leads* to that union whereby I become one with him and call upon the Father.

A realization of his loving presence also leads to friendship, a friendship rooted in that last discourse where the beloved disciple lay close to the breast of Jesus and heard him say: "You are my friends. . . . No longer do I call you servants . . . but I have called you friends . . ." (John 15:14, 15).

Friendship with Jesus has played a central part in the lives of thousands of Christian mystics who have experienced Jesus walking beside them as he walked beside the disciples going to Emmaus, or who have experienced him living in them as he lived in Paul. With Peter they have said: "Yes, Lord; you know that I love you" (John 21:16). They have spoken to the Lord about their hopes and fears, about their plans and projects, about their successes and failures, about their joys and sorrows. They have realized that he is the friend of friends, the faithful one who will not let them down. They have realized that this is the friendship in which all other friendships are rooted.

Intimacy with Jesus has also been central to the lives of thousands, even millions, of simple Christians who have knelt before him asking for daily bread and for help in their difficulties.

But now I hear you again. You ask about social problems and nuclear war. You complain that this Jesus-and-I spirituality is a cop-out, a flight from the urgent problems of our explosive world.

Well, it could be a cop-out. But properly understood this prayer has a profoundly social dimension. For if my friendship is authentic, I will be concerned not only with my problems but also with his. And we know that Jesus is concerned with the poor, the sick, the oppressed, the downtrodden, the underprivileged, the despised. Not only is he concerned with them; he identifies with them. If we want to be his friend, we must also be their friend. If we want to be his friend, we must open our hearts to his presence in the vast world of suffering and injustice and oppression. Friendship with Jesus is friendship with the world.

### III

Let me here pause to say that this loving involvement with Jesus, the Risen Lord, is the very essence not only of Christian mysticism but of the Christian life. This needs to be said. Alas and alack, so many Christians think that the Christian life consists in keeping the rules. Or they think that faith consists in subscribing to the correct formula. How far they are from the gospel and from the kingdom! How Paul would have torn his hair, if he had hair!

It is good to reflect that the Council spoke of faith as a total commitment to God who reveals and it deliberately got away from the idea that faith means assent to a series of propositions.[1] When this commitment is made in a radical way it leads to an altered state of consciousness which is truly mystical.

And do not think that I am throwing church law out the window. It surely has its place. I only say that to make law the center of the Christian life is contrary to the gospel, where total commitment to Jesus beyond any rule or law is the one thing necessary.

## IV

I hear you say: "Intimacy with Jesus! Friendship with the Risen Lord! This is beautiful and beautifully Christian. But is it mysticism? Surely mysticism means entering the void, the cloud of unknowing, the emptiness, the darkness, the nothingness; whereas the prayer you describe is full of words, thoughts, images, pictures, emotions. How can this be mysticism?"

Let me first describe this prayer. One may pour forth one's heart to the Lord in words. Or one may repeat some form of the Jesus prayer or whatever. But eventually this leads to a silence whereby one rests in his loving presence without words. And in this silence there may be no picture, no thoughts, but only a simple sense of presence, of love, of union. Indeed, if you ask someone who prays like this, "What does Jesus look like?" the person cannot answer because he or she has no mental picture of Jesus but only a rich feeling that Jesus is lovingly and peacefully present—perhaps like warmth or light. Here there is an altered state of consciousness. Here there is mysticism.

But apart from this, I must say something sharp and direct:

You don't understand the void! Many people don't understand the void. They have no experience; and they think that the void or the cloud means blotting out all images, getting rid of thought, making one's mind a blank—becoming a zombie!

Now this is not the void. In zen, for example, one can enter the void while listening to the sound of the waterfall or watching the falling peach blossom or looking at the murmuring stream or attending to the flow of one's breath. *The void is constituted by detachment, nonattachment, nonclinging—not by blotting things out.* In the void I do not cling to thought; but I may think. I do not cling to words; but I may use words; I do not cling to pictures but I may have mental pictures. In short, the void is not an annihilation of thinking and feeling and imagining (if it were that, Christians would rightly reject it) but a purification of all these.

St. Teresa of Avila entered into the void and she saw Jesus therein. I believe the two disciples going to Emmaus entered into the void, into an altered state of consciousness, when they talked to Jesus and later said: "Did not our hearts burn within us while he talked to us on the road, while he opened to us the scriptures" (Luke 24:32). The void is no mere negation (even though it is often described in negative terms) but a state of consciousness full of spiritual wealth.

## V

In Christian tradition, as Moses was the great mystic of the Old Testament, Mary of Bethany was the great mystic of the New. From the time of Augustine and before, Mary sitting at the feet of Jesus was the model of the mystics. Great was her love for Jesus; even greater was his love for her. Here we have intimacy; here we have union; here we have mysticism.

The author of *The Cloud*, highlighting this famous scene, writes of Mary:

Neither did she notice our Lord's human bearing, the beauty of his mortal body, or the sweetness of his human voice and conversation. . . . But she forgot all this and was totally absorbed in the highest wisdom of God concealed in the obscurity of his hunmanity.[2]

Now let me here be frank. While I love and admire the author of *The Cloud,* the above statement does not make me happy. The author implies that Mary forgot the humanity of Jesus and was preoccupied with his divinity. Here I detect a neoplatonic flight from the body (we know that the English author belonged to the Dionysian tradition) and a certain fear of the senses. Perhaps the author feared an erotic interpretation of this beautiful scene.

How different is the approach of St. Teresa of Avila! She never wants to forget the humanity of Jesus, however deep her mystical experience; and *for her this is possible because of her doctrine of interior senses.* Nor is this just her doctrine; it is found in a whole tradition going right back to Origen who speaks of "the heavenly sensuality of those experienced in prayer."

This doctrine is found preeminently in St. Ignatius who loves to introduce us to a world of inner seeing, hearing, smelling, touching, tasting, savoring. This is no world of pure spirit. It is a world of flesh and blood, albeit of transformed, transfigured flesh and blood. Ignatius loved the *Anima Christi* wherein the inner senses shine forth brilliantly, even shockingly. "Blood of Christ, inebriate me" runs the prayer; as though one were to cry:

"Blood of Christ, make me drunk!"

And it goes on:

"Hide me within thy wounds!"

Surely these words have no meaning outside a mystical world of transfigured sensation.[3]

Joined to this, Ignatius had a strong sense of history. After his conversion he wanted to go to the Holy Land. He wanted to see the place where Jesus Christ lived and died. He was aware of the most minute details. And when he asks us to kneel at the foot of the cross to be inebriated with the blood of Christ and to hide within his wounds, Ignatius is keenly aware that *this cruci-fixion really happened.* What a combination of history and mysticism! What a sense of the reality of the Incarnation!

Let me add a word. I write these pages in the Philippines at a small village outside Manila. Around me I have seen simple people touching and kissing statues of Our Lord. I have seen them rubbing the statute with their handkerchiefs and then rubbing the same handkerchiefs all over their bodies and the bodies of their children. I know that this shocks some visitors. But to me it is profoundly Christian, and it even contains an element of mysticism—mysticism of the senses. The people are immersing themselves in the humanity of Jesus. The sense of touch is deeply significant for them. Blood of Christ inebriate me! Hide me within thy wounds!

### VI

The church fathers loved to quote the words of Paul: "But put on the Lord Jesus . . ." (Romans 13:14). Here Paul is asking us to put on Jesus as we put on a garment—to be clothed with him. And later authors ask to be naked of self and clothed with Christ.

And being clothed with him we identify with him in his death and resurrection. Union with Jesus is not something static but a living out of the Pauline ideal "that I may share his suffering, becoming like him in his death that if possible I may attain the resurrection from the dead" (Philippians 3:10, 11). And in Romans Paul writes: "If we have died with Christ, we believe that we shall also live with him" (Romans 6:8). And in Galatians: "I have been crucified with Christ . . ." (Galatians 2:20).

As the eyes of Jesus were always fixed on the Father, so are the eyes of one who says: "It is no longer I who live but Christ who lives in me" (Galatians 2:20). And so, as friendship develops it leads to identification with the one we love. Identified with Jesus and filled with the Spirit, we cry out: "Abba, Father!" Now we have entered with Jesus into the inner life of the Trinity. Here is the apex of Christian mysticism.

## VII

Christianity, then, is intensely human and intensely incarnational. Paul, great mystic that he was, tells the Corinthians that he "decided to know nothing . . . except Jesus Christ and him crucified" (1 Corinthians 2:2). John, the mystical eagle, soars to heaven with his eyes fixed on Jesus: for in Jesus he sees the Father. Francis of Assisi, Ignatius of Loyola, Teresa of Avila—they all soar to heaven not by forgetting Jesus but through him, with him, and in him.

For this human Jesus born of the Virgin Mary is also divine. He invites us to share in his divinity, to become children of God, to enter the very life of the Trinity, where with him and in the Spirit we cry out: "Abba, Father!"

I said that the word *mysticism* was originally associated with mystery. And what mystery is more sublime than this?

## NOTES

1. *Dei Verbum* C.1, 5; *The Documents of Vatican II*, ed. Walter M. Abbot (New York: American Press, 1966), p. 113.
2. *The Cloud of Unknowing and The Book of Privy Counselling*, ed. and trans. William Johnston (New York: Doubleday Image Books, 1973), chap. 17, p. 71.
3. For a development of this theme, see my *The Mirror Mind* (San Francisco: Harper & Row, 1981), chap. 6.

# 10

# Eucharistic Mysticism (1)

I

I have said that in Christian mysticism one may not deliberately forget the humanity of Christ: we cannot sidestep the Incarnation. If we do, we may eventually forget not only the humanity of Jesus but everyone's humanity, including our own. We may find ourselves forgetting the Jesus who is in the poor and the sick and the oppressed. We may forget the whole social dimension of Christianity in favor of a vague, cosmic religion of pure spirit which tries to go directly to the godhead.

"I see this in theory," you say. "But I am perplexed. Are you trying to push me back to the old discursive prayer with its images and pictures of Jesus? Besides, where is this humanity of Jesus? Where can I find him?"

Here we get some help from the Council. Speaking about the work of redemption, it outlines the modes in which Christ is present:

> To accomplish so great a work, Christ is always present in His Church, especially in her liturgical celebrations. He is present in the sacrifice of the Mass, not only in the person of His

minister, "the same one now offering, through the ministry of priests, who formerly offered Himself on the cross," but especially under the Eucharistic species. By His power He is present in the sacraments, so that when a man baptizes it is really Christ Himself who baptizes. He is present, finally, when the Church prays and sings, for He promised: "Where two or three are gathered together for my sake there am I in the midst of them" [Matthew 18:20].[1]

Now draw the practical conclusion from the above. Jesus is present in the Eucharist. He is present when you read the Bible, including the Old Testament. He is present in the community where two or three are gathered in his name. He is also present (though the Council, speaking in a liturgical context, does not here mention the fact) in the hungry, the thirsty, the naked, the imprisoned. You may have no picture of him. You may not be able to describe him. You may say in astonishment: "Lord, when did we see thee hungry and feed thee, or thirsty and give thee drink?" (Matthew 25:37). You may recognize his presence only through naked faith. But believe that he is really there. *As his presence is mystery, so an experienced grasp of his presence is mysticism.*

In this chapter I would like to reflect on his presence in the Eucharist. I believe that this is a real presence. The Eucharist is a symbol but it is also the reality: it is a symbol which contains the reality. One thing is sure: Christians have always believed that it is the body of Christ—not just his soul, not just his divinity, but also his body.

## II

Let me begin with the primitive Christian community. Whatever definition one gives to mysticism, it is impossible to deny that the first disciples underwent profound mystical experience. It all began when Jesus was crucified. This was their dark,

dark night, when their grief and depression knew no bounds and they were brought to the brink of despair. But as the mother who was in travail is flooded with ecstatic joy at the birth of her child, so the sorrow of Calvary turned into the overwhelming joy of the resurrection and the ascension, reaching a great climax at pentecost. In all this, the disciples were filled with the unrestricted love that goes on and on and on. Their consciousness was expanded when suddenly they recognized him in the breaking of bread or standing by the sea. Their experience needed no proof for it was total and self-authenticating. Above all, through this series of shocks they underwent profound conversion of heart. Transformed and changed out of all recognition they fearlessly proclaimed the good news. Who can doubt that the earliest Christian experience was intensely mystical?

At the Last Supper, his farewell meal, Jesus had taken bread and blessed and broke it saying, "This is my body which is given for you. Do this in remembrance of me." And likewise the cup after supper saying, "This cup which is poured out for you is the new covenant in my blood" (Luke 22:19, 20). At that time Jesus, foreseeing Calvary, accepted his death as the offering of himself to the Father for the redemption of the world. Now, after his ascension, his disciples, faithful to his word, gathered together to break bread and to remember that saving event. When I say "remember" I do not mean that they recalled something that happened in the past but that *they made the event present.* This was the re-membering which brought Christ in his redemptive act into their very midst so that subsequent generations would speak of "the real presence," would believe that the bread and wine are changed into the body and blood of Christ, and would chant the anamnesis:

> When we eat this bread
> And drink this cup

> We proclaim your death, Lord Jesus,
> Until you come in glory.

I said the Christians gathered for the breaking of bread. They also told the story of Jesus and later this story became the New Tesament. And it was the combination of word and sacrament and loving community that created the mystical experience, a mystical experience of the individual and of the group.

And in all this let me again underline the historical dimension of Christian mysticism. The Christian community did not, and does not, bring about a repetition of what happened on Calvary. "For we know that Christ being raised from the dead will never die again; death no longer has dominion over him" (Romans 6:9). What happened in history once and for all enters into our place and our time—and it will do so until the Parousia, or Second Coming. Such is the incarnational and historical dimension of the Christian mystical experience.

But, alas, human nature is not always geared to mysticism. Already in the early days, the meal in Corinth became rowdy and unmystical. Paul scolds his spiritual children vigorously: "When you meet together it is not the Lord's supper you eat. For in eating, each one goes ahead with his own meal, and one is hungry and another is drunk" (1 Corinthians 11:20, 21). And then, recalling the night on which Jesus was betrayed, Paul insists on the reverence with which one should eat and drink, lest one profane the body and blood of the Lord.

And through the centuries the Christian community has remembered-and-made-present the mystery of Christ. At times this had been, and still is, a powerful mystical experience. At other times, as in Corinth, "each one goes ahead with his own meal, and one is hungry and another is drunk." And so it will be until he comes in glory.

III

"But now you upset all my ideas," you say. "You turn me upside down! I thought of my mysticism as a very spiritual experience: you say it is incarnational and you even associate it with eating! I thought of mysticism as outside time and space: you focus on an event which took place at a specific time in a specific place. I thought of mysticism as intensely individual and solitary: you associate it with a community. You shock me!"

I hear what you say. As I write this book I realize more and more that Christian mysticism is indeed unique. But let me make a few points of explanation.

First of all, a mysticism of eating is not foreign to Asia. Think of the aesthetic and spiritual dimension of the Chinese cuisine. Think of the Japanese tea ceremony. Westerners in the seventeenth century were astonished and amused that Japanese should develop an art and a spirituality of drinking tea.

And in the Jewish tradition also we find a mysticism of the meal. I myself had some experience of this when I was invited to share a paschal meal with some Jewish friends in Jerusalem. The father blessed his children; he read Exodus and explained it to them while they cheerfully asked questions. We drank our four glasses of wine and enjoyed a family meal. Then I realized existentially that eating can be a religious experience. I got an inkling into that paschal meal at which Jesus instituted the Eucharist.

Again, at Qumran, I visited the ruins of the Essenes' dining room with the lectern where a monk read the Bible to the assembled community. Then I recalled how in the Christian monastic tradition also the refectory was a holy place, a place of silence where the Scriptures were read while the community ate. And, interestingly enough, something similar is found in Buddhist monasticism.

Eating, ordinary eating, is sacred for two reasons. First, because it is a celebration of death and life. The fruits of the earth die in order to come to life within us and as part of us. Second, the meal is sacred because it is a sign and a pledge of the friendship and love that exists between those who eat together.

It is not surprising, then, that Jesus should carry out a large part of his public ministry at meals. It is not surprising to see him feed the five thousand. It is surprising, but beautifully surprising, to see him eat with tax collectors and sinners. The meals about which we read in the gospel all point to that supreme banquet where Jesus says: "I am the bread of life" (John 6:48) and, "Truly, truly, I say to you, unless you eat the flesh of the Son of man and drink his blood, you have no life in you" (John 6:53).

And so we celebrate the mystical banquet: "Your fathers ate the manna in the wilderness, and they died. This is the bread which comes down from heaven, that a man may eat of it and not die" (John 6:49, 50). For many Christians the moments after receiving the Eucharist are profoundly mystical. They savor and taste the bread of life; they become aware of the extraordinary union of love that exists between themselves and their Lord. With Paul they cry: "It is no longer I who live, but Christ who lives in me . . ." (Galatians 2:20). Now they know that their true life lies hidden with Christ in God. Now they can say: "For me to live is Christ, and to die is gain" (Philippians 1:21). Now they feel that they are being transformed so that Jesus comes to see through their eyes, to hear through their ears, to bless through their hands, to love through their hearts. I here spell out in words what they feel; but the actual experience may be one of total silence, an intensely felt presence, a loving union, a mystical ecstasy.

IV

The Eucharist has both a personal and community dimension. And today we feel drawn more and more to emphasize the community dimension, to emphasize with Paul that "because there is one bread, we who are many are one body, for we all partake of the one bread" (1 Corinthians 10:17), to stress with John that Jesus is the true vine and we the branches.

In fact the Eucharist has always been the key to Christian community, since it forms a bond which is far beyond the natural love of human beings one for another—or perhaps it is more correct to say that it transforms the natural love of human beings one for another. This has been particularly evident in monastic and religious life where "the community liturgy" has been the key to everything. Through the community liturgy a real mysticism of interpersonal relations has slowly developed. And when I say a real mysticism I do not mean that communities have always enjoyed a rich sense of God's loving presence. From what I have said in this book it will be clear that absence, abandonment, anxiety, depression, struggle, failure, and dark night are built into mysticism. And this holds true not only for the individual but also for communities.

We know that whole communities pass collectively through dark and harrowing nights. If they then knew what was happening! If they then knew that their darkness and suffering is a very real experience of God's presence! If they knew this, they might pass triumphantly through death to resurrection, as the apostolic community passed through the anguish of Calvary to the joy of Pentecost.

Here I speak of community mysticism in monastic life. Until our day this eucharistic mysticism of community has been little developed in lay communities and in married life. But we are now in an age of the laity, an age when we know that all Christians are called to holiness and to mysticism; and the time has come for us to investigate and to live out a eucharistic mysticism of lay community and of family life. This is surely one of the great challenges of our day.

And let me add one word. Aquinas describes beautifully how the Eucharist is the center of Christian sacramental life—all the sacraments, he says, point towards it. I myself always had difficulty in seeing how the sacrament of matrimony points towards the Eucharist. Only now do I get some inkling. For the Eucharist is the body of Christ and, properly understood, it will lead us to a whole theology of the body and even of sexuality. Moreover, the Eucharist is the key to community; and what community is more vital in human life than the family?

## V

> For from the rising of the sun to its setting my name is great among the nations, and in every place incense is offered to my name, and a pure offering; for my name is great among the nations, says the Lord of hosts. [Malachi 1:11].

The church fathers loved to quote the above words from the prophet Malachi, applying them to the eucharistic sacrifice which from East to West is always offered to the Father for the redemption of the world. At any given moment the great event of salvation is somewhere remembered-and-made-present; and the faithful have been encouraged to pause for a moment in a busy day to unite themselves with this earthshaking event.

In the early days the Eucharist was reserved after the celebration to be brought to the sick and dying. And today we still have the beautiful word *viaticum* meaning "food for the journey," the journey of death. Christians, moreover, were permitted to retain the sacred species in their homes for this purpose. From this there naturally developed the custom of revering

and honoring and adoring the Eucharist, though this custom
became widespread only from the ninth century. Then came the
feast of *Corpus Christi* (the Body of Christ) with eucharistic
processions and prayer before the Blessed Sacrament. About
this I shall speak at greater length in the next chapter. Here
only let me say that reservation of the sacrament gave a great
incentive to Christian prayer and Christian mysticism.

Yes, I hear what you say. You have read that this medieval
eucharistic piety was too individualistic, that it separated the
body of Christ from the liturgical celebration, that it encouraged a static devotion to Jesus while overlooking *the event* which
is the very core of his redemptive work.

There is some truth in all this. However, it simply reminds us
that misunderstanding and abuses always creep into religious life
and that reformation is always needed. For eucharistic piety *need
not* be individualistic, as I have repeatedly pointed out. And it
*need not* neglect the great event of our salvation. For whenever
one looks at the tabernacle wherein the sacred species are reserved, one can recite the anamnesis: "Christ has died; Christ
has risen; Christ will come again." In other words, one can
recall the whole mystery of Christ, not just his static and individual presence.

Let us not forget that prayer before the tabernacle has nourished the spiritual life of millions of Christians. Even today if
you visit a church in Manila or Belfast, in Tokyo or Hong
Kong, you will find people kneeling in silent prayer. Often this
is prayer of petition; or it is thanksgiving; or it is that familiarity
with Jesus that I described in the last chapter. Sometimes people recite the rosary, recalling the mystery of Christ in the company of the Virgin Mary; sometimes they use no words but relish
and taste that the Lord is sweet. This is indeed a prayer of the
people, of the masses of the people.

"But," you say, "is it scriptural? Is it found in the New Testament?"

To this I answer that as there is a development of doctrine within Christianity, so there is development of religious experience. No sensible theologian thinks that we should preach to modern New York or Tokyo exactly what Paul taught to Corinth. Everybody knows that doctrines develop and change and are adapted as they enter new cultures and as, under the guidance of the Spirit, the community gets new insights. If we were to maintain that people today should pray and sing and celebrate liturgy as did the early Christians, we would get bogged down in a biblical fundamentalism: we would lose the richness which Christianity possesses precisely because of its universality, its openness to all cultures, its willingness to make progress and to develop.

Obviously we need norms to test the validity of later developments and adaptations. Let us recall (and let theologians recall) the old theological adage, *lex orandi: lex credendi*: the way of praying is a norm of faith. The word of God is found not only in the Scriptures but also in the living faith and worship of the masses of the people in union with their shepherds.

## VI

But does the eucharistic community isolate Christians? Does it separate us from the world community of Jew and Moslem, Buddhist and Hindu, agnostic and atheist? Does it separate us from men and women of science, from all those who have no faith in Jesus and his risen presence?

Again, this is a challenge we Christians have not yet adequately faced. Ideally, the eucharistic community is a sign of the unity of all men and women. Ideally, it should point to, should lead to, unity and peace among all peoples and nations. That we have not yet succeeded in living the Eucharist in this powerfully unifying way is all too clear. This is yet another challenge for tomorrow.

### NOTE

1. *Sacrosanctum Concilium* C.1, 5; *The Documents of Vatican II*, ed. Walter M. Abbot (New York: American Press, 1966), p. 113.

# 11

# Eucharistic Mysticism (2)

I

I once heard a Zen Master lecture on Buddhist and Christian symbolism. He spoke of the Buddha on the lotus as the central Buddhist symbol and of Jesus nailed to the cross as the central Christian symbol. Afterwards, having occasion to speak with him, I said that while the cross is undoubtedly a great Christian symbol, Christianity has a more important symbol, namely, the Eucharist. For while the cross speaks of the death of Jesus, the Eucharist speaks not only of his death but also of his resurrection and second coming: *Christ has died; Christ has risen; Christ will come again.*

The point is important. Every student of religion knows that symbols are of the very essence of religion and of mysticism. Symbols, and symbols alone, can carry us to mystical levels of awareness and to states of consciousness which are completely unknown to dry, discursive theology. I used to think naively that Zen Buddhism was without symbols because of its stress on emptiness and nothingness and "no dependence on words and letters." Now I realize that the very emptiness and nothingness are symbols as also are the lotus posture and the rhythmic breathing. Now I know that Zen is full of symbols.

One of the characteristics of the Judeo-Christian tradition is that the most important symbols are also historical events or historical persons. The Eucharist is a symbol and it is also the reality: the body of Christ. It is the true bread, the true manna which came down from heaven and gives life to the world.

Bread is indeed a powerful symbol. Alas, those who live in the first world do not appreciate bread because they have it in abundance and have never experienced hunger. Let them go to the third world. Let them see people undernourished, people starving, people desperate because they have no bread for their children, then they will realize that every scrap of bread is precious. Then they will appreciate the delicate command of Jesus: "Gather up the fragments left over, that nothing may be lost" (John 6:12). The children of Israel, starving in Sinai, appreciated the gift of bread; and the gospel tells us that what they, and we, really desire is the true bread which gives eternal life. This is Jesus who makes the extraordinary claim that "he who comes to me shall not hunger, and he who believes in me shall never thirst" (John 6:35).

## II

Now there is a way of prayer which consists in being present to the symbol. To be present to the symbol does not mean thinking about the symbol or forming a picture of the symbol or even staring at the symbol. In Asia, where the art of presence is highly developed, one can learn to sit cross-legged, to breathe from the abdomen, to still the mind, to fix one's attention on a single object or a single point—and in this way to be totally present to the symbol. This is presence of mind and body and spirit; this is presence of conscious and unconscious mind. What a wonderful art!

But even without this art one can be totally present through love. For love engages the whole person drawing all the faculties, conscious and unconscious, to the one we love.

And in a Christian context one can learn to be totally present, lovingly present, to a crucifix or to an ikon or to a text of Scripture or to the greatest symbol: the Eucharist. Now we are present not to an object but to a person, to a loving person who has died for us. He engages not only our mind but also our heart—our affective life, our love, our all. United with this person and with the drama in which he is the chief actor we are transformed (forgive me for saying it again) and cry out with Paul: "It is no longer I who live, but Christ who lives in me" (Galatians 2:20).

Such is the symbolism of bread. But I find another richly symbolic aspect to the Eucharist. Before speaking about it, permit me by way of a disgression to say something about the *mandala* in Asian thought.

## III

The word *mandala* means circle. Sometimes the circle is empty: at other times it contains all kinds of buddhas and bodhisattvas. Hindus and Buddhists regard it as a source of great psychic energy. Indeed, there is a saying attributed to the Buddha: "When you fix your heart on one point, then nothing is impossible for you." When one fixes one's heart on the mandala then one becomes very, very powerful.

The mandala can be used in many ways. One can be totally present to the mandala, thus using it as an aid to meditation. Or one can draw one's mandala daily, watching it change and develop. Or one can dance the mandala. Or one can form the mandala with one's body, as happens when one adopts the Lotus posture forming the "cosmic mudra" with thumbs lightly touching while the arms form a beautiful circle. Again, prayer beads are a mandala as also is the Asian prayer wheel. In all these cases the symbolism of the circle is of the greatest significance.

I said the mandala is a source of great psychic energy. Now let me say that this energy flows chiefly in two areas.

First, the circle is a symbol of integration, of wholeness, of perfection, and finally of enlightenment. Underlying this is the realization that human nature, inwardly torn and divided, is in great need of healing. We are all wounded because of the imbalance between the *yin* and the *yang*, between the unconscious and the conscious, between the feminine and the masculine. By being present to the mandala, by interiorizing it, by *becoming* it, we attain to psychic wholeness and to enlightenment.

Zen masters claim that they can gauge the degree of a person's enlightenment from the circle he or she draws. Conversely Jung, who sometimes got his patients to draw mandalas, claimed that he could gauge the degree of sickness or health from a person's mandala. I might add in passing that for some years Jung drew his own mandala each day and saw reflected therein the picture of his own psychic development. He also claimed that as the Buddha is the center of the Buddhist mandala, so Christ is the center of the Christian mandala. And Christians who like to draw the mandala sometimes confirm Jung's intuition.

Second, the mandala is a cosmic symbol. By interiorizing the symbol I break out of my narrow individuality, becoming one with the circle and one with the universe. In India the mandala is sometimes a symbol of God.

When I became interested in the Asian mandala and then looked at my Christian heritage I began to see mandalas everywhere. It was as though Christian artists and theologians had stumbled on this powerful symbol without being explicitly aware of its inner psychological dynamics. And so I saw mandalas in the stained glass windows of the great cathedrals as well as in the rosary beads. Theologically I saw a mandala in the Thomistic doctrine that through contemplation we who are wounded and divided in *the state of fallen nature* return by a cyclic process to *the state of integrity* or *the state of innocence*—the state of our first parents who, in paradise, were naked and unashamed. Here, too, the circle is a symbol of healing, of wholeness, of integrity.

However, through this apparent digression, I am leading to something highly significant. I believe that the Eucharist, particularly when circular bread was used and placed in the monstrance before the people, became the great Christian mandala.

Do not misunderstand me. I realize that the shape of the bread is not of central importance. What matters is the body of the Lord, the true bread which came down from heaven. Nevertheless, granted that faith is the central thing, it is also interesting to reflect that the ordinary laws of psychology are at work. If it is true (and I believe it is) that the circle is a source of psychic power to integrate and to make cosmic, then the use of the monstrance and the circular eucharistic bread was a great insight and a great step forward in the history of Christian religious experience. Let me say more about this.

## IV

In primitive Christianity, as I have already said, the Eucharist was primarily a liturgical act by which the community remembered-and-made-present the sacrificial meal of Jesus with his disciples. "Dying you destroyed our death; rising you restored our life; Lord Jesus, come in glory."

In the thirteenth and fourteenth centuries, however, there arose new forms of eucharistic piety which were to exercise the most profound influence on Catholic prayer and worship from that time until this very day. It all began with the desire of the people, the masses of the people, to gaze on the body of the Lord with faith and love and devotion. Put in modern terms, *they wanted to fix their eyes on the symbol*. And the bishops, partly because they saw this as a response to certain Christological and eucharistic errors and partly because they saw it as the work of the Spirit in the people, encouraged the celebrant to raise the Sacred Host after the consecration.

This custom spread rapidly throughout Europe; and we hear of pious people running enthusiastically from church to church to be present at the elevation of the host and to gaze lovingly at the body of the Lord. Nor was this devotion confined to the common people. In 1210 the bishop of Paris had ordered the Sacred Host to be elevated; and in the same year this custom was adopted in all Cistercian monasteries. And in 1222 it was prescribed for the Carthusians. In England and France there arose the custom of hanging a black curtain behind the altar so that the white host would stand out clearly against the dark backdrop. Later came the custom of making the prayer, "My Lord and my God" as one gazed on the elevated host—and this custom has survived until our day.

In 1215 the doctrine of transubstantiation, formulated by Peter of Lombard in the twelfth century was defined by the Fourth Lateran Council. And in 1264 the feast of *Corpus Christi*, which had been celebrated locally, was extended to the universal church. With it came processions and prolonged eucharistic prayer.

In the fourteenth century the monstrance or *ostensorium*, in which is enthroned the Blessed Sacrament, first appeared in France and Germany; and again this eucharistic devotion was greeted with enthusiasm and spread throughout Europe like wildfire. The making of the monstrance became a fine art. Some were made as statues of Jesus; others of Mary holding the host in upraised arms. Some were very ornate and elaborate; others were so large that they were carried through the streets in carts. Today the custom of prayer and meditation before the monstrance is deeply rooted in the Latin Church and in those countries influenced by the Latin Church. From Manila to New York and from Dublin to São Paolo this eucharistic prayer is a devotion of the masses of the people.

And the Eucharist enthroned in the monstrance has all the properties of the mandala. One is present to it, totally present. One interiorizes it by eating or (if this is not possible) by a spiritual communion in which by ardent desire one receives the body of the Lord into the depths of one's being. As one assimilates the Eucharist one is filled with the most tremendous energy—for the bread is food not only for the body but also for the spirit: "Truly, truly, I say to you, unless you eat the flesh of the Son of man and drink his blood, you have no life in you" (John 6:53). And this bread of life is medicinal, healing, leading to integration of the personality, pointing beyond *the state of integrity* to the resurrection, which is *the state of glory*.

Again, the Eucharist is a cosmic symbol. Through reception of this sacrament we are united not only with the individual Jesus but with the whole Christ. We are united with those who have gone before us, with those in the state of purification, with the poor and the sick and the oppressed; for all are his members. Indeed we are united with the whole human family each of whom is related to the risen Lord in a way that surpasses human understanding.

## V

Now let me come to a practical point.

Everyone knows that throughout the Christian world there is a longing for deep meditation—not for discursive meditation—

but for the quiet contemplative prayer that leads to deeper states of consciousness. Put more clearly, there is a longing for mysticism.

Now I submit the thesis that the answer to this yearning is the Eucharist. Moreover I submit the thesis that the monstrance is of central importance. In the past the faithful have prayed vocally: now they can be encouraged to pray silently. For our time I believe it is good to have a very simple circular monstrance in which the Blessed Sacrament is exposed. It can be placed on a low table; and people who like to sit cross-legged or in the lotus posture or on a low prayer stool, regulating their breath and stilling their mind, can do so. In any case they can learn to be totally present to the symbol—just being—remembering that in this case *being* equals *being-in-love*. When this is proposed, my experience and the experience of others is that ordinary people glide into deeper states of consciousness with the utmost ease.

Needless to say, we must recall that the eucharistic presence is a prolongation of the liturgical drama: "Christ has died; Christ has risen; Christ will come again." "It is no longer I who live but Christ who lives in me." "Abba, Father!" We can remain without words in a total and loving presence.

## VI

I have spoken of total presence to the symbol, of interiorizing the symbol, of becoming one with the symbol; and all this means total presence to the Lord, interiorizing the Lord, becoming one with the Lord. Now following on this one can make a prayer of offering, a prayer whereby, united with Jesus, one offers oneself to the Father in the Spirit. I spell it out in words but the offering can be made in wordless silence.

Here let me say that prayer of offering is eminently eucharistic. This is because the Last Supper was a sacrifice in which

Jesus offered himself to the Father for the salvation of the world. The church stressed this point and spoke of the Eucharist as the fulfillment of all the sacrifices of the Old Testament beginning with that of Abraham, who was willing to sacrifice his son, Isaac.

During the eucharistic liturgy the faithful have always been encouraged to offer themselves with Jesus. As a sign of this they sometimes carry in procession to the altar the bread and wine which will be offered during the sacrifice, as well as other gifts symbolizing the offering of their hearts and their lives. In this way they are encouraged to offer their whole selves to the Father.

Now this offering, made briefly during the eucharistic celebration, needs to be prolonged. And I might say in passing that this is one more reason for reserving the Eucharist in the tabernacle or in the monstrance: simply that the time of liturgy is short and mystical experience takes time. Sometimes for one flash of loving insight one must spend fifty minutes of boredom. Consequently the time of liturgy alone will not ordinarily suffice for mysticism. But let me return to the prayer of offering.

As I have said, this offering can be made while one sits before the monstrance interiorizing the Eucharist so that the mystery of Christ is not just "out there" but also "in here." And now, one with Jesus or clothed with Jesus, I offer myself to the Father for the salvation of the world. Such prayer is very traditional. Take, for instance, the well known prayer of Ignatius *Sume et suscipe* ("Take and Receive"), a prayer which I myself now take in a eucharistic context. This is an act of total offering and it can be an act of mystical offering. Let me explain.

Early in the *Spiritual Exercises* Ignatius speaks of a discursive prayer wherein one freely uses one's memory, understanding, and will. But now, at the end, he proposes something different. Now he says in effect: "Lord, take my memory—*I will not remember*. Take my understanding—*I will not think*. Take my will—*I will make no colloquy*." And in this way I am brought into silence, into mystical silence, without words or reasoning or petition. Now I enter a new state of awareness where words are no longer necessary. Yet I do not reject words and phrases. Rather do I say: "If you want me to remember, make me remember. If you want me to think, make me think. If you want me to petition, make the petition within me." This is the summit of *wu-wei* or nonaction, the summit of letting God act. This is the true void. Here is mysticism at its height.

And so again we have in the presence of the Eucharist a prayer of total silence—but now of silent or blind offering. It is a silence which is Trinitarian, since one with Jesus I offer myself to the Father in the Spirit. If words do escape my lips they will likely be: "Abba, Father!"

In a similar vein there developed over the past few centuries the pious custom of daily offering one's total self—prayers, works, actions, sufferings—to the Father in union with the eucharistic sacrifice of Jesus. This was known as the morning offering. Followed through in a radical way it could lead to high mysticism. It is furthermore interesting to recall that the Council, speaking of the universal vocation to holiness, points to martyrdom as the supreme offering and the supreme testimony of love:

> From the earliest time, then, some Christians have been called upon—and some will always be called upon—to give this supreme testimony of love to all men and women, but especially to persecutors. The Church, therefore, considers martyrdom as an exceptional gift and as the highest proof of love. . . . By martyrdom a disciple is transformed into an image of his Master. . . .[1]

Since these lines were written many Christians have offered their lives not only in the traditional style of martyrdom but also as martyrs for social justice. Surely this total holocaust is the apex of eucharistic mysticism: the offering of one's all to the Father in union with Jesus.

## VII

For the bread is broken. Jesus took bread and blessed and broke and gave to his disciples. This is no mere convention. The eucharistic bread is broken because Jesus was broken when he died on the cross and the martyrs were broken when their blood flowed out on the parched earth. And we also are broken in order to be healed and remade.

As the eucharistic mandala is broken, it points towards an even more mysterious mandala: the Trinity. The old theologians spoke of the circle of *circumincessio*, the circle of the indwelling of the Son in the Father and the Father in the Son and of both in the Spirit. We also enter into this cyclic process in accordance with those words of Jesus in the fourth gospel: "In that day you will know that I am in my Father, and you in me, and I in you" (John 14:20). And it is through the Eucharist that we enter into the Trinity—identified with the Son we live in the Father and in the Spirit. In this way the Eucharist leads to the ultimate and eschatological mandala which is the Trinity.

### NOTE

1. *Lumen Gentium* C.5, 42; *The Documents of Vatican II*, ed. Walter M. Abbot (New York: American Press, 1966), p. 71.

# 12

# Mysticism
# and Life

I

One of the great religious problems of our day is the cleavage between prayer and life. We all know of pious people who patronize the church on Sunday; who swindle, cheat, and exploit the poor from Monday till Saturday; and who kneel piously in the pews on the following Sunday. Nor are the mystics exempt from such aberrations. Here we must be honest. Look at history and you will see clerics, mystical people, who were cruel, unjust, ruthless, and unscrupulous in daily life—and then they went devoutly to their morning *prie-dieu*, blotted the whole thing out, and piously entered the cloud of unknowing. Alas and alack for the weakness of human nature! In varying degrees we all do this. We blot out of consciousness the things we don't want to see.

Jung speaks of *the shadow*. This is not just our evil side. It includes *everything we do not want to see*. We love the darkness. "And this is the judgment, that the light has come into the world, and men loved darkness rather than light because their deeds were evil" (John 3:19). Even the most consummate mystic has his or her shadow, his or her blind spots, his or her unregenerate areas. To have a shadow is part of the human condition: it is a consequence of what we call original sin.

This, then, is a problem we must confront in the life of prayer and the life of mysticism. And what I want to suggest in this chapter is eminently practical. I say: *Let life flow into your prayer and let prayer flow into your life.* Be open in prayer. Face your shadow. Do not blot things out. Take them in and be present to life when you are present to God. Learn the great art of being present to God, to yourself, and to life.

## II

As an example of one who was present to God, to herself, and to life, I propose the Virgin Mary as she appears in the pages of the third gospel. Here we read that Mary and Joseph came down from Nazareth to Bethlehem, where Jesus was born. And Luke writes: "But Mary kept all these things, pondering them in her heart" (Luke 2:19). What was Mary pondering in her heart? No doubt the journey from Nazareth, the rejection of Jesus at the inn, the birth of the child, the visit of the shepherds. Her life was flowing into her prayers. She was turning over in her heart the happenings of these days. This is not discursive prayer: it is a savoring, a tasting, a relishing, a wondering, a contemplative presence to God, to self, and to life.

And at the end of the same chapter a similar sentence occurs. Jesus had been lost. Mary and Joseph, after a three-day search, found him in the temple. And his mother (was she angry? or just bewildered?) complained: "Son, why have you treated us so?" (Luke 2:48). And Jesus answered: "How is it that you sought me? Did you not know that I must be in my Father's house?" (Luke 2:49). And Luke ends the chapter by telling us that "his mother kept all these things in her heart" (Luke 2:51).

They did not understand. Nor were they the first parents who could not understand their child. "How is it that you sought me?" This was like a zen *koan*. How could they not seek him?

Mary kept these things in her heart. Her life was flowing into her prayer; and she lived in silent wonder.

And was the whole life of Mary a similar prayer? When Simeon said that a sword would pierce her soul, when she followed Jesus in his public life, when she stood at the foot of the cross—was she constantly pondering these things in her heart? The Lukan portrait of Mary, the mystic, would suggest that this indeed was so.

For the prayer of Mary was penetrated with yet another mystical word: *Fiat*. "Behold, I am the handmaid of the Lord; let it be to me according to your word" (Luke 1:38). It was as though she said: "Let God act; I will not put obstacles in His way; I welcome His action; I will cooperate." And this word *fiat* echoed in her heart as she pondered the events of life.

With this *fiat* something momentous happened not only in Mary's womb but also in her mind and heart. An inner revolution took place as she accepted her vocation and her destiny. And her greatness is precisely here. Remember how, much later, a woman raised her shrill voice in the crowd and shouted to Jesus: "Blessed is the womb that bore you and the breasts that you sucked!" But he said, "Blessed rather are those who hear the word of God and keep it" (Luke 11:27). He was saying that the sanctity of Mary was not just in her physical maternity but in her total acceptance of the word of God. *Fiat*.

I believe that the *fiat* is the key to mysticism. It is the Christian version of the Taoist wu-wei or noninterference. "Let life flow at its deepest level. Let the forces of the universe act. Let God act. I will not fight against His will."

And the *fiat* came swiftly and spontaneously to the lips of Mary because of a prior enlightenment: "Hail O favored one, the Lord is with you" (Luke 1:28). Hearing these words Mary knows that she is loved, uniquely loved and lovable. She is without sin. And with the realization of God's love for her came the loving and trusting response of love for God. *Fiat.* Let it be done.

### III

We are all invited to imitate the prayer of Mary. We can all ponder in our hearts the happenings of daily life and utter our fiat. Such prayer can be a modification of the prayer of quiet. It is as though there were two levels of psychic life or two states of consciousness existing at the same time. At one level we enjoy the obscure sense of presence and union—this is the level of the true self. And at another level the events of life are flowing in and out in an unstructured way.

Now it is all-important to remain attentive to God's presence at the deepest level. Do not *cling* to the events of life. Let them come and let them go, while you remain with God.

Literally anything can come into this kind of prayer; our joys, our sorrows, our anxieties, our successes—our temptations however sordid, our failures however humiliating, our hopes however sublime. Sooner or later our shadow will painfully surface; and if we face it squarely in God's presence we will come to the joy of self-acceptance and enlightenment.

Into this prayer come our neuroses, fears, hang-ups. Sometimes in this psychological age one hears: "Solve your psychological problems first and pray afterwards!" As if the gospel were for the psychologically healthy! In fact the gospel (and consequently Christian prayer) is for the neurotic, the psychotic, as well as for the sinner. Anything can come into the prayer and anything can be healed.

Again, the life of the senses can flow into this prayer. By this I mean the sound of the wind, the heat of the sun, the roar of the waves, the rustle of the leaves. I can walk through the forest aware of every sound, present to life, present to myself, present to God.

Or again, some people take their dreams into this prayer of pondering. It is not a question of interpreting the dream or understanding it, but rather of being present to it while, at a deeper level, I am present to God.

Now this kind of contemplation may sound very simple; and simple it is. But it can also be demanding. For if with Mary I am uttering my *fiat*, if I am surrendering to the deeper forces within me, if I am surrendering to God, then I am losing control. I am handing over to another. "It is no longer I who live but Christ who lives in me." And, of course, we all like to be in control; we all like to run our own ship. Where am I going? Where is this prayer leading me? What a risk! Now I am like Peter, to whom the Lord said: "Truly, truly I say to you, when you were young, you girded yourself and walked where you would; but when you are old, you will stretch out your hands, and another will gird you and carry you where you do not wish to go" (John 21:18).

We can be sure that as the fiat effected a profound revolution in Mary, so it will effect a profound revolution in us. This revolution is nothing less than metanoia or conversion of heart.

## IV

This Marian contemplation is valuable for decision making. Again, one enters the state of consciousness where God is present; and into this void one brings the matter for discernment. It is not a question of searching for an answer but of being present and allowing the decision to be made (perhaps over a period of weeks or months) at the depths of one's being, at the level of one's true self.

And let me here pause to say that such contemplation is eminently suitable for the laity. We live in an age when Christians have to make decisions, sometimes agonizing decisions, in areas of economic, political, social life—decisions which may affect the lives of millions of people. Now there was a time when devout Christians asked the institutional church to make their decisions and the institutional church felt obliged to do so. But those days are gone. The Council speaks clearly of "the autonomy of earthly affairs" saying that the temporal order has its own laws in which the church is not competent. Concretely it advises the lay person:

> Let not lay people imagine that their pastors are always such experts, that to every problem which arises, however complicated, they can readily give them a concrete solution, or even that such is their mission. Rather, enlightened by Christian wisdom and giving close attention to the teaching authority of the Church, let lay people take on their own distinctive role.[1]

This short passage is in fact revolutionary. It indicates that we are moving out of the age when the institutional church could lay down the law on every subject, telling people what to do. We are now in an age of conscience. We are now in an age when people must make their own decisions. In this age the role of the institutional church is to teach the gospel and *to teach the people to pray and to discern.* Nor is ordinary prayer enough. Only through mystical prayer can people attain to the inner freedom whereby they will see what is right and have the courage to do it.

V

Again, this Marian contemplation can be of immense value for those who work in situations of extreme poverty and oppression. We all know that those who see exploitation, oppression, and injustice before their very eyes undergo great struggles. If you see innocent people beaten, humiliated, tortured, degraded by police and military; if you see them misrepresented by the press and calumniated by the establishment, what do you do? Some people get wild with anger: they cooperate with terrorism and join a campaign of bombing. Others get depressed and discouraged: they lose all hope. Others are paralyzed by fear. Others are attracted to a false ideology which perverts or twists the gospel. Others pray and let this painful situation flow into their prayer. What agonizing prayer! Now it is almost intolerable to sit still.

In these circumstances, let us remember that Mary pondered things in her heart as she saw her son unjustly condemned and crucified. What agonizing prayer! How difficult it was to utter that *fiat*! And we, too, if we ponder these things in our hearts, if we can be quiet when all hell breaks loose inside us, then the *fiat* will come; and it will bring new energy, new hope, new strength—not the energy and hope and strength which come from human nature but the energy and hope and strength which come from God. For the *fiat* is dynamic. It would be an abysmal understanding to think that *fiat* means: "Let the injustice and the oppression and the murder continue." It does not mean that. It means, "Let God act. Let God act within me at the deep, mystical level. Let the universe act. I will cooperate with the immense power deep in me and in the universe." What revolutionary energy is here!

## VI

"But," you say, "is this mystical prayer? Can there be a mystical prayer wherein the content is the humdrum events of life or economics or civil war or oppression or the work in which I am engaged? Surely one forgets all this in authentic mystical experience."

Some mystics forget everything. But others do not. Take, for example, St. Ignatius. Towards the end of his life he was writing *The Constitutions of the Society of Jesus*. If you or I were writing such a book we might say to ourselves: "When I go to pray I'll speak to God and forget about my book. I'll bury it beneath a cloud of forgetting. To think about it would be a distraction. Let me put it out of my mind and talk to God."

But Ignatius did not do this. Those constitutions were the warp and woof of his prayer, day after day. And while discerning about what he should write or not write he had abundant tears, visions of the Trinity, visions of Mary. Read his *Spiritual Diary*. It is a remarkable document showing the most profound coexistence of earth and heaven, of practical action and sublime mysticism.

But why speak of Ignatius when the same thing can be found in St. Paul? Read the introduction of his epistles and you find that love for his flock and anxiety about his churches was the core of Paul's mysticism. "And so, from the day we heard of it, we have not ceased to pray for you, asking that you may be filled with the knowledge of his will . . ." (Colossians 1:19). In Paul there was no schizophrenic cleavage between his relationship with God and his relationship with people. It was all one. Life was flowing into his prayer as his prayer flowed into life.

## VII

I have spoken about how the happenings of daily life can flow into our prayers as they flowed into the prayer of Mary. Now let me add another aspect of this Marian contemplation, an aspect that is peculiar to our day.

We know that in this century the human race has undergone a change of consciousness: we now share in what I might call a universal or global consciousness. By this I mean that we become increasingly aware of the joys and sufferings of the whole of humanity in a way which was impossible for St. Ignatius or St. John of the Cross or even for St. Paul.

Now the Council encourages Christians to develop in themselves this consciousness of the world and this concern for the whole human family. The magnificent opening sentence of the document, *The Church Today*, runs as follows:

> The joys and the hopes, the griefs and the anxieties of the men and women of this age, especially those who are poor or in any way afflicted, these too are the joys and hopes, the griefs and anxieties of the followers of Christ.[2]

Here and elsewhere the Council asks us to resonate with the world while fostering in our hearts a sensitivity and a compassion for the poor and afflicted everywhere.

Now this affects prayer. It means that as prayer develops and as consciousness expands, we come to ponder in our hearts not only our own personal joys and sufferings but also the joys and sufferings of the whole world. Concretely, the oppression of the poor, the torture of the innocent, the agony of the third world, the injustice of the first world, the danger of nuclear war, the pollution of the atmosphere—all or any of these may enter into our prayer. The true follower of Christ has a heart that is open to the whole world. "Mary kept all these things pondering them in her heart."

But let me be realistic. The suffering of the world is immense; and each one of us cannot take responsibility for all that pain. Perhaps what is asked of us is a certain openness whereby we allow the Spirit to bring to our awareness those problems about which we should pray at any given time.

I hear you say: "That sounds fine. But what can I do about it? Little me? I am helpless in the face of such misery. Why should I worry my head off and make myself sick?"

And yet, even if you cannot do anything practical you can *suffer with* (this is the root meaning of compassion) and this is a value in itself. This was the prayer of Mary: a suffering with her son. And in our day such compassion does in fact achieve much. What we need is a conversion to justice and compassion on the part of a significant number of people. We need ten just men and women who will influence the collective unconscious, ten just men and women who will influence the Teilhardian *nousphere.* This is more important than the frenetic activity of thousands of others.

## VIII

I hear you say: "But what about the cloud of forgetting? Does not the author of *The Cloud,* a writer you love and admire and about whom you have written profusely—does he not tell the contemplative to bury every single creature beneath a cloud of forgetting and go to God in naked silence?"

Quite frankly, I am not so enthusiastic about the cloud of forgetting as I once was. Yet I believe it is justifiable for several reasons.

First of all, forgetting everything is a transitional stage of purification. It is a time when one is liberated from clinging in order to remember with detachment and serenity.

Again, if while you are prayerfully pondering things in your mind and heart—if at this time you are swept into a cloud of unknowing, forgetting everything and present only to God, by all means follow that call. In a certain sense you forget everything, but in another sense you are present to the world in a new way. Some people, solitaries or hermits, are called precisely in this way. True, they forget the social suffering of the world, but they come up against the very source of evil in the dark night. This vocation I respect. I have written about it already in this book. I believe it is the sublime vocation of few people.

Finally, as life flows into prayer, so prayer must flow into life. The loving presence of God experienced in mystical prayer can be experienced also in the hurly-burly of life. The anguishing absence of God experienced in mystical prayer can be experienced in the hurly-burly of life. This is the ideal of contemplation in action.

### NOTES

1. *Gaudium et Spes* C.4, 43; *The Documents of Vatican II*, ed. Walter M. Abbot (New York: America Press, 1966), p. 244.
2. Ibid.; ibid., p. 199.

# 13

# Mysticism
# and Poverty

I

"Blessed are the poor . . ." These words welled up from
the depths of his being. They were the very core of his message.
"How happy are the poor! How really blessed are the poor!"

Exegetes have asked about the meaning of this gospel poverty. Some have said that the poor were the masses of the
people in the Roman Empire who had to work in order to live.
Others say that Jesus spoke of the *anawim*, those who, feeling
their utter helplessness, relied only on God. *I myself believe that
Jesus spoke primarily about himself.* And for this reason his words
have power. If a bloated capitalist were to pull on his cigar and
say that the poor are blessed, we would smile. But Jesus said it.
He was talking out of his own experience of poverty and ecstatic
joy. "How happy are the poor . . . !" This is the Jesus who was
born in poverty, the Jesus for whom there was no room in the
inn, the Jesus who had nowhere to lay his head. Above all, this
is the Jesus who emptied himself, taking the form of a slave,
who cried out, "Eloi, Eloi, lama sabacthani." And this same
Jesus, out of the depths of lived experience, cries: "How happy,
how blessed, how blissful are those who are poor!"

Such was the great mystical experience of Jesus. It was utterly radical in nature. It was a process which began in Bethlehem and reached a great climax on the cross when he emptied himself in a total kenosis. And he experienced the joy and the bliss of resurrection when God highly exalted him and bestowed on him the name which is above every name, "that at the name of Jesus every knee should bow in heaven and on earth and under the earth, and every tongue confess that Jesus Christ is Lord, to the glory of God the Father" (Philippians 2:10).

And the followers of Jesus share in his experience. They too become poor, radically poor: they too are exalted. Think of the Virgin Mary who in the third gospel can speak of her kenosis saying that "he has regarded the low estate of his handmaid" only to add:

> For behold, henceforth, all generations will call me blessed.
> [Luke 1:48]

And the same pattern is found in Abraham who is willing to lose everything, even his son Isaac, and is exalted so that by his descendants all the nations of the earth shall bless themselves. Again, it is found in Peter who has left everything but will receive the hundredfold. Yes, the person who sells everything and gives to the poor in order to follow Jesus has blissful joy, has the most profound mystical experience. Such is the gospel promise.

And subsequent history confirms this. Think of Francis of Assisi who stripped himself naked, handed his clothes to his father, and said that his true Father was in heaven. How Francis loved the Lady Poverty! What joy he found in her sweet company! The mystical joy of radical poverty is a fact of experience. How often we hear people say that their time in prison—when they were oppressed and deprived of everything—was the happiest time of their life. In the very moment of total loss they experienced the exhilarating joy of resurrection. In losing their lives they found their lives.

Nor is there anything inhuman in this total loss. The fact is that as life goes on we must all lose everything. We grow old; we are stripped; we die. And if we accept this loss of all we find the joy of resurrection, not just after death but also here and now. Such is the pattern of human life. How happy are those who are poor!

## II

In this book I planned to write little about Buddhism. Nevertheless I would like here to say a word about that great religion which has helped me understand more richly my Christian heritage.

Buddhist poverty is radical. One way of meditation is to sit cross-legged and recite the word *mu* with the exhalation of the breath. *Mu* means *nothing*; and as I breathe, I empty myself of clinging to all things. (Please note that I do not empty myself of all things but of clinging to all things.) And so I let go of clinging to material things such as money and possessions, of clinging to thinking and reasoning and rationalization, of clinging to my desire for revenge, to my pride, covetousness, lust, gluttony, envy, anger, and sloth. And now there comes a great liberation and a great enlightenment. Such is the joy of possessing nothing.

It should be noted that the great enemy is not money and possessions but covetousness, which can be a vice of rich and poor alike. As long as we covet things and cling to them we cannot be happy, as long as we multiply our needs we cannot be at rest, because these needs become so many burdens, so many chains keeping us in bondage. The gospel constantly warns us not to hoard—not to be like the man who builds bigger and bigger barns and then dies in his sleep. "Fool! This night your soul is required of you . . . " (Luke 12:20). This story makes sense to Buddhists. They understand well how Paul, once liberated, can call himself "poor yet making many rich, as having nothing yet possessing everything" (2 Corinthians 6:10).

The Christian, like the Buddhist, can pray with *mu*. His or her prayer can be a total self-emptying while awaiting the joyful enlightenment of resurrection. Christian prayer, however, will differ from that of the Buddhist in that it is Christocentric. I empty myself in imitation of Jesus, in the company of Jesus, in love for Jesus. This emptying is a putting on of the mind of Christ Jesus who emptied himself taking the form of a slave and was exalted, so that every knee bows at the mention of his name. Indeed this is the process outlined by St. John of the Cross who speaks graphically about *all and nothing (todo y nada)*. This is a living out of the gospel truth that in losing our life we find our life.

And there is another prayer of poverty suitable for Christians. One can simply sit cross-legged, empty, and naked before God. One is without words, without possessions, without thoughts, just being. Now one recognizes one's total poverty. Now one can cry from the heart: "Blessed are those who know that they are poor!" In the existential recognition of my own poverty I find enlightenment and strength. With Paul I exclaim: "When I am weak then I am strong" (2 Corinthians 12:10).

### III

From all this it will be clear that the poverty of the gospel is not just economic poverty but a total emptiness, a total liberation from clinging. The first beatitude is all-embracing. The oppressed, the captives, the persecuted, the blind, the handicapped, the underprivileged, all are poor.

Now sometimes theologians have tried to rationalize evangelical poverty and to show that the teaching of Jesus makes sense. Futile endeavor! This is like trying to explain the cross which, Paul tells us, is supreme foolishness. One will come to an understanding of evangelical poverty not by rationalization but by treating it as a Zen koan.

Concretely, entering into a deep state of consciousness, I take the words "Blessed are the poor" into the very depths of my being. I become present to them. This is not a question of rationalization but of presence. And as I turn them over in contemplative fashion I begin to feel the wonder of it all: I even experience shock. Until now my unconscious belief was, "Blessed are the rich," but here is a totally different story. I remain with the words until I finally identify with them, become one with them, live them. Now in a flash I feel convinced that the poor are blessed because I am poor and I am blessed. Now I realize that Jesus was poor and Jesus was happy; Mary was poor and Mary was happy. Now I know beyond all doubt that this saying is true. Now I grasp the text not because I understand it rationally but because I live it. Or, more correctly, *I understand the text through life.*

And let me refer to one more Buddhist insight.

Buddhists have a saying that emptiness equals compassion. This means that poverty equals compassion. I empty myself totally in order to receive the whole universe into my heart (Eastern Buddhists say into my *hara* or belly) with an immense compassion. And this Buddhist saying can also be Christian. Jesus emptied himself, taking the form of a slave in order to save sinful men and women. The salvation of the human race is rooted in the compassionate poverty of the Son of God.

Likewise evangelical poverty leads to compsssion or *is* compassion. If we want a norm for the authenticity of our poverty here it is: Does my Christian poverty lead to compassion for suffering people everywhere?

## IV

When we see the centrality of poverty in the gospel story we understand how thousands upon thousands of dedicated men and women through the centuries have vowed themselves to a life of total poverty. Imitating the kenosis of Jesus they make a vow to live this most radical mystical life with its suffering and its immense joy.

"Beautiful theory," you say. "But the facts are different. Already in my short life I have met lots of discontented monks and religious who don't understand their vow of poverty. They say they are not poor by any standards. They feel guilty. They want to exchange their vow of poverty for a vow of simplicity. Besides, the church is scandalously rich. Even in third world countries, the church and religious orders own lots of property and land. Sometimes they remind me of multinational companies; and, worst of all, they have a reputation for paying low wages to their employees. All you say about mysticism is fine, beautiful, wonderful; but it just doesn't fit the facts."

I hear you. And it is not easy for me to respond. But let me try.

First, about the monks and religious who are ill-at-ease with regard to their vow of poverty. Alas, it is true that the mystical dimension of poverty was lost. I believe that much responsibility lies with the canon lawyers and moral theologians. They wanted to delineate clearly the meaning of poverty. *They wanted rules.* They wanted to tell the religious what he or she could or could not do. They wanted to tell us what was sinful and what was lawful. They were uncomfortable with mystery and they had little understanding of mysticism. The notion of process was absent from their laws. I cannot recall that they said anything about the link between poverty and compassion.

And so, observation of the vow of poverty degenerated into fidelity to the rule of poverty. "Keep the rule and the rule will keep you" was the great slogan. And the rule told people to turn in their earnings faithfully to the treasurer, to ask scrupulously for permissions, not to have superfluities. Wonderful rules! But what about the mystical joy of kenosis? What about compassion? Small wonder that many modern religious do not know what poverty is about. And the answer?

The answer is a renewed and authentic understanding of the New Testament. We find the answer when we identify with that man who found the treasure in the field and who *with great joy sold everything to buy the field.* That man was a mystic. Again, the answer is to see the life of poverty as a process whereby one becomes more and more poor as Jesus became more and more poor. It is a gradual losing of all things reaching a great climax in death and resurrection.

Your second comment about the wealth and power of the church is even more painful. It reminds me of the fact that we are all weak and sinful and that the followers of Christ commit the same sins as other people in our day. Let me first say a word about how we got into this mess.

The spirituality of the Bible is eminently communitarian. Religious experience is experience of the people; love of God is the love of the people; the Eucharist is the sacrament of the community; sin is the sin of the people. What counts is the community.

As Christianity developed in the West, however, the individual or personal dimension of religious experience was more and more stressed; and it was particularly stressed in the field of mysticism. Whereas the bride of the Song of Songs represented originally the people, the community, the church, she came to represent the individual soul searching lovingly for her bridegroom. In itself this was not a bad thing. But the sad truth is that the community dimension of spirituality and particularly of mysticism was obscured and even lost.

And all this had great repercussions on the approach to poverty. In religious orders the poverty of the individual was legalistically stressed, but the poverty of the institution was forgotten. We forgot that the community, the institution, the church, no less than the individual, have a mystical vocation to imitate the Jesus who emptied himself, taking the form of a slave. Only in the last two decades have we become acutely aware of the need for communal poverty in the modern world. Only now do we become aware of the value of institutional virtue and the evil of institutional sin.

Here the Latin American bishops give courageous example to the universal church. They see that recognition of our sinfulness is the necessary basis for change:

> The Latin American bishops cannot remain indifferent in the face of the tremendous social injustices existent in Latin America, which keep the majority of our peoples in dismal poverty, which in many cases become inhuman wretchedness . . . and complaints that the hierarchy, the clergy, the religious are rich and allied with the rich also come to us . . . Many causes have contributed to create this impression of a rich hierarchical church. The great buildings, the rectories and religious houses that are better than those of the neighbors, the often luxurious vehicles, the attire inherited from other eras, have been some of those causes.[1]

The bishops go on to say that a very great number of parishes and dioceses are in fact extremely poor and that many of the clergy live in complete deprivation. Yet they confess:

> Within the context of the poverty and even of the wretchedness in which the great majority of the Latin American

people live, we, bishops, priests and religious, have the necessities of life and a certain security, while the poor lack that which is indispensable and struggle between anguish and uncertainty.[2]

They then ask for a conversion of heart, a new commitment to the poverty of Jesus, a commitment to the poverty of compassion whereby the person with two coats shares with the person who has none. Nor is it sufficient that this be a conversion of the individual. It must be communal. We must become the church of the poor as Jesus was the friend of the poor. Interesting too is their appeal to the masses of the people:

A sincere conversion has to change the individualistic mentality into another one of social awareness and concern for the common good. The education of children and youth, at all levels, beginning in the home, ought to include this fundamental aspect of the Christian life.[3]

This conversion from an individualistic mentality to a mentality of social awareness is surely one of the greatest challenges not only to Christians but to all men and women interested in the survival of the human family.

And obviously this appeal of the bishops is particularly relevant for people living in the first world. For it is no secret that the affluent countries are exploiting the third world with harsh brutality. They are, as the Council observed, "hypnotized by economics;" and only a conversion to the poor will save us from global disaster.

In the first world a step in the right direction is the growing "exposure to the poor." Opportunities are given for people to see the grinding poverty and misery of the oppressed masses; opportunities are given for people to see the frightening consequences of nuclear war; statistics are available showing the billions of dollars spent on arms while millions die of hunger. If all this information flows into the prayer of Christians, bringing about a profound conversion of heart, we can have hope for the future.

### V

I hear you say: "You talk about conversion of heart. You talk about mystical emptiness in imitation of Jesus who emptied himself, taking the form of a slave. And you ask this not only from the individual but also from the community. You ask for conversion not only of the businessmen in Wall Street but even of the clerics in the Vatican. Surely this is not realistic. Surely this is a romantic dream."

If this is a romantic dream, then Christianity is a romantic dream. For this is the core of the Christian message. I realize that we are weak. I realize that we are particularly weak in all that concerns money. I realize that we all have our lapses and always will. But if we lose sight of "Blessed are the poor . . ." then we betray the gospel of Jesus Christ. Christianity is a radical religion, a mystical religion. Let us not water it down.

Realistically I see that the whole world will not be converted nor will all Christians. But if a significant number of people change their hearts and dedicate themselves to the poor, they can change the world. Remember the ten just men who could have saved Sodom. "Then he said, 'Oh let not the Lord be angry, and I will speak again but this once. Suppose ten are found there.' He answered, 'For the sake of ten I will not destroy it'" (Genesis 18:32).

Let us pray that ten just men and women will be found in the first world lest it succumb to the fate of Sodom.

### NOTES

1. Joseph Gremillion, *The Gospel of Justice and Peace* (New York: Orbis Books, 1975), p. 471.

2. Ibid.
3. Ibid. See also the 1968 Medellín Conference Documents in *The Church in the Present-Day Transformation of Latin America in the Light of the Council* (Washington, D.C.: United States Catholic Conference).

# 14

# Mysticism
# and Peace

I

On the slopes of the Mount of Olives a small Franciscan chapel marks the spot where Jesus wept over the city he loved. "And when he drew near and saw the city he wept over it, saying, 'Would that even today you knew the things that make for peace'" (Luke 19:41).

I loved to come to this hallowed place to enjoy the panoramic view of Jerusalem and to cast my mind back over those centuries pregnant with history. At the center of all stands the resplendent Dome of the Rock built magnificently by seventh-century Moslems on the very spot where Solomon constructed his beautiful Temple of cedarwood and gold. Here also stood the second Temple, the wonderful stones and the wonderful buildings towards which Jesus and his disciples turned their prayerful gaze. "Do you see these great buildings? There will not be left here one stone upon another that will not be thrown down" (Mark 13:2). Then the El Aqsa Mosque, the Antonia Fortress, the Tower of David. Further back the Church of the Holy Sepulchre which commemorates Golgotha and the heartrending

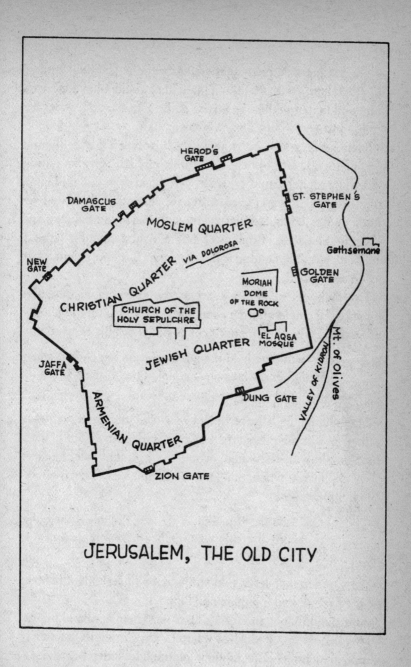

JERUSALEM, THE OLD CITY

*Lama sabacthani.* What vibrations from the past! What history! "O Jerusalem, Jerusalem . . . How often would I have gathered your children together as a hen gathers her brood under her wings, and you would not!" (Luke 13:34).

I reflected on Jerusalem's bloody history of four millennia. City of David, city of peace, the holy city, the city away from which a prophet cannot perish! Jerusalem was besieged more than fifty times, conquered thirty-six times and destroyed ten times. It was conquered by Egyptians, Assyrians, Babylonians, Persians, Seleucids, Romans, Moslem Arabs, Seljuks, Crusaders, Saracens, Mameluks, and Ottomans. But two events stood out in my mind.

The first was in 587 B.C. when the Babylonians destroyed Solomon's Temple of cedarwood and gold, dragging the Jews off into exile. Sadly the Hebrew poet writes about his beloved city:

> She weeps bitterly in the night, tears on her cheeks; among all her lovers she has none to comfort her. [Lamentations 1:2]

Alas, for the desolate city!

The second equally terrible event was in A.D. 135 when Jerusalem was mercilessly sacked by the Roman legions, when the Temple was desecrated, when the holy city was renamed *Aelia Capitolina,* when the Jews were banished from their beloved city forever:

> O God, the heathen have come into thy inheritance; they have defiled thy holy temple; they have laid Jerusalem in ruins. [Psalms 79:1]

Small wonder that Jesus told the women of Jerusalem to weep for themselves and for their children.

And the unhappy situation today! Jerusalem is carved up into a Jewish quarter, a Moslem quarter, an Armenian quarter, a Christian quarter. The Church of the Holy Sepulchre itself, traditional site of Calvary, is divided up between Greek Orthodox, Franciscans, Armenians, Syrians, Copts, and Ethiopians, a division effected by the ruling Turks in 1757 because Christians were quarrelling fiercely among themselves. And so there is tension between Jews and Moslems, between Moslems and Christians, between Jews and Christians, between Christians and Christians.

Then the terrorist bombs. The armed soldiers frisking civilians in the streets, stopping cars, climbing on buses. "O Jerusalem, Jerusalem . . . !"

## II

My thoughts moved from Jerusalem to another divided city: my native city of Belfast. Often as a child with my father I climbed the Cave Hill, counterpart of the Mount of Olives, and looked down on the drab city almost hidden by a pall of smoke. The Catholic Falls and the Protestant Shankhill. The Union Jack and the Tricolor. "No Pope here." "Remember 1690." "Join the I.R.A."

Even at that time Northern Ireland was a vicious police state, and I knew that I belonged to a repressed and underprivileged minority. But today! The inhuman atrocities of the army and the police: the equally inhuman response of the terrorists. The bombs, the snipers, the booby traps, the maimed, the blind, the armless, the legless. The soldiers smashing down doors and ripping the insides out of televisions in their search for guns. The lethal rubber bullets leaving children wounded and dying in the streets. The explosions in pubs and dancehalls. The senseless sectarian killings. The assassination squads of the British army. The secret interrogation centers. The horrendous prison conditions, the sophisticated and brutal torture. The men on the blanket. The dirty protest. The agonizing hunger strike. The heartless intransigence of Margaret Thatcher. The cruel death

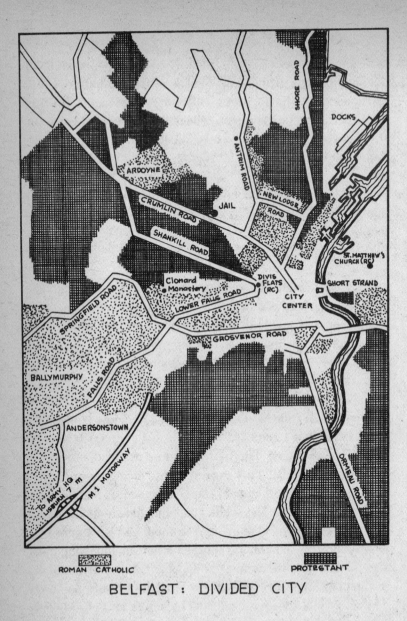

ROMAN CATHOLIC          PROTESTANT

BELFAST: DIVIDED CITY

of Bobby Sands. And on top of all, the massive unemployment, the grinding poverty, the institutionalized contempt for human rights. "And when he drew near and saw the city he wept over it saying, 'Would that even today you knew the things that make for peace'" (Luke 19:41).

But why do I speak of Jerusalem and Belfast? Think of the division from Berlin to Tehran, from Kampuchea to South Africa, from Warsaw to Kabul. Think of the violence in the streets of Chicago and New York. Think of the racial riots in London. And then you will realize that Jerusalem is a symbol of a world divided. Yes, the whole world is a Jerusalem, a global city where superpowers have created a fear of nuclear destruction, a global city cruelly divided between the wealthy north and the impoverished south, the starving many and the affluent few. "And when he drew near and saw the city he wept over it . . . " (Luke 19:41).

I have heard it said that the situation in Jerusalem is hopeless. No solution! I have heard it said that the situation in Belfast is hopeless. No solution! I do not believe this. If the situation in Belfast and in Jerusalem is hopeless, then the situation in the whole world is hopeless. For the problem is everywhere the same.

### III

We all know that the basic problem is neither Jerusalem nor Belfast nor Moscow nor Washington. The basic problem is the human heart. "For from within, out of the heart . . . come evil thoughts, fornication, theft, murder, adultery, coveting, wickedness, deceit, licentiousness, envy, slander, pride, foolishness" (Mark 7:21). Wise old Jung reflecting on the awful happenings of the 1940s spoke of an unconscious psychic epidemic, vicious and brutal, stalking Europe like the black death of the dark ages; and one wonders if we are still in the throes of a psychic epidemic infinitely more pernicious than the black death. The Preamble of the Constitution of UNESCO clearly recognizes the psychic dimension of our predicament: "Since wars begin in the minds of men and women, it is in the minds of men and women that the defense of peace must be constructed."

All this is obvious and recognized by everyone. But how are we to heal the human mind and heart? We can heal broken legs and we can rebuild cities. But what about the mind?

*The gospel tells us that the human mind and heart are healed only through metanoia.* And the gospel is clear about the reasons for the destruction of Jerusalem. It says nothing about the economic, political, and military background. It says nothing about the awesome and ruthless power of the Roman legions against which the fanatical zealots could not stand. It says nothing about the arrogance of Vespasian and the cruelty of Titus. For underlying all this was a more fundamental problem:

> You were not faithful to the covenant
>
> or
>
> You did not change your hearts
>
> or
>
> "You did not know the time of your visitation" (Luke 19:44).

Yes, the central problem was metanoia or change of heart.

This is the message of the gospel and, indeed, of the whole Bible. Jesus was following an Old Testament tradition when he said that infidelity to the covenant brings destruction. "Woe to you, Chorazin! woe to you, Bethsaida! for if the mighty works done in you had been done in Tyre and Sidon, they would have repented long ago, sitting in sackcloth and ashes" (Luke 10:13). They would have repented; they would have changed their hearts.

The problem then, the root problem, is conversion of heart.

And vis-à-vis the modern world the gospel throws out the same challenge: "Do you want to avoid a nuclear holocaust? Do you really want peace? If so, change your hearts."

Divided city. Strumpet city. The harlot. The faithless one. Sodom and Gomorrah. Belfast. Jerusalem, Moscow, Dublin, Washington. Tokyo. London. Beijing. Cairo. The message is the same. "Unless you repent you will all likewise perish" (Luke 13:3).

## IV

On the Mount of Olives I discovered a Zen temple. It was constructed by Nakagawa Soen whom I met at Mishima where he lives in an exquisite little temple called *Ryutakuji*. The Master felt that the holy city should have a Buddhist presence to complement the teachings of Jews, Moslems, and Christians. Modest and unassuming, the tiny temple is situated on the top of the hill. On one side, the Mount of Olives sweeps down to Jerusalem; on the other, the Judean wilderness sweeps down to the Dead Sea. The Master said with wry humor that his temple was close to the Dead Sea but atop the mountain of "O Live!"

But the panoramic view was not apparent from the dimly lit meditation hall where I sat for several hours with four Israelis and the Japanese teacher.

At first I was surprised to find a Buddhist temple there. I was even shocked. It seemed out of place. What was a Zen temple doing in the city of David, the city of Jesus, the city whence Mohammed ascended to heaven? But the longer I sat the more I realized that Zen has an important message for the monotheistic religions.

For the fact is that Zen abhors all divisions, abhors all use of the discriminating intellect, abhors all words (*no dependence on words and letters* is the great slogan) whereas the divisions and wars and quarrels among the monotheistic religions have been caused primarily by our clinging to words, to letters, to dogmas, to formulas, to structures, to doctrines. If only we could soar above all these formulations to meet the living God, Yahweh, who is our common Father. If only we could meet the God to whom the formulations point. If only we could move towards a mystical state of consciousness where all is one. Alas, instead of that, we have fallen into an idolatry of doctrines; we have judged people's orthodoxy by whether or not they subscribe to the correct formula; we have burned people at the stake because they did not use the right words. How much better if we judged orthodoxy by love of God and neighbor!

And Zen goes not only beyond words and letters but beyond fear, anxiety, greed, pride, lust, envy, anger. It goes to the serene atmosphere of unity, to the reconciliation of opposites, to the oneness of being. It has its change of heart, its metanoia, its *satori*.

Now what I say of Zen is true also of Christian mysticism. It also leads to an altered state of consciousness where all is one in God. If we are faithful to the gospel we will come to see that words and letters (even the most sacred words of the Bible) are no more than a finger pointing to the moon. Let us look at the moon which is God and let us join hands with Jews and Moslems whose eyes are fixed on the same God—the God of Abraham, of Isaac, of Jacob. Let us rise above that evil sectarianism which has wrought such havoc in Jerusalem, in Belfast, in Rome, and in Geneva.

Lest there be any misunderstanding, let me here add that I am not against words. They have their place. Without the finger we cannot see the moon. My point is that we have divinized words; we have made the relative absolute. Only by passing from a discursive, wordy Christianity to a mystical and supraconceptual Christianity can we authentically find God and authentically love our non-Christian brothers and sisters in a world that is fast becoming one.

V

About Christian conversion of heart I have already spoken at length. I have said that it consists in fidelity to the covenant, whereby we accept God's love and love in return. "We love because he first loved us" (1 John 4:19). I have said that fidelity to the covenant includes fidelity to the gospel teaching that the poor are blessed. Practically, I asked you to take the koan "Blessed are the poor," to become present to the words, to turn them over in your mind, to relish them, to be baffled by them, to live them until (perhaps after weeks or months or years) a tremendous inner revolution takes place whereby you become poor, you identify with Jesus poor, you experience the ecstatic joy of kenosis. Only then can you say that you understand the text.

Now in the same way I propose the koan "Blessed are the peacemakers for they shall be called the children of God" (Matthew 5:9). Read what the exegetes say (God bless them!) and learn all you can. But do not stop there. Become present to the words, turn them over in your mind, relish them, be baffled by them, live them until (perhaps after weeks or months or years) a tremendous inner revolution takes place whereby *you become a peacemaker, you identify with Jesus the peacemaker, you experience the ecstatic joy of being a peacemaker.* Now you understand the text at a new level of consciousness, at a mystical level of consciousness where all is one in Jesus.

You say: "But I need no great conversion in this area. I long for peace as do millions of others. What is this great revolution you talk about?"

You say you long for peace. And I believe you. But are you willing to pay the price? Pope John wrote an encyclical letter called *Peace on Earth (Pacem in Terris)* and, lo and behold, he said almost nothing about war and peace: the whole letter was about justice, about respect for the human dignity of every person and every group of persons in the whole world. We all say we want peace (and we certainly do fear nuclear war) but, if we are serious, we must make the sacrifices so that fewer people die of hunger, fewer people live in subhuman conditions, fewer people have their human dignity flaunted and trampled into the ground. A conversion to peace includes a conversion to justice, to poverty, to the whole Sermon on the Mount, so that we turn the other cheek, love our enemy, do not resist the evil one, give away our cloak as well as our coat. Ay, there's the rub! What a revolution in consciousness! You and I have still a long way to go.

"All right," you say. "I have a long way to go. But I still have problems. If this is the real meaning of 'Blessed are the peacemakers' how come Christians took so long to understand the text? How come the Church preached the crusades, encouraged wars, threw holy water on guns and battleships? And there is the scandalous fact that Christians have been fighting among themselves for centuries."

Yes. Some things in our history make me blush. Christians have sinned like everyone else. But let me say a word about the background.

The early Christians loved peace and were troubled in conscience about serving in the Roman Imperial army. St. Maximilian was martyred because he refused military service. St. Martin of Tours remained in the army until called upon to kill in battle and then refused to do so. Tertullian (155–240) declared that in taking Peter's sword Jesus disarmed every soldier. Listen to Origen (185–254):

No longer do we take the sword against any nation nor do we learn war any more since we have become the sons of peace through Jesus . . .[1]

For Origen, Christians help the Emperor not by the sword but by their prayers. In short, in primitive Christianity there was a mystical and eschatological approach to peace, a belief that peace is God's gift as it was the farewell gift of Jesus: "Peace I leave with you, my peace I give to you . . . " (John 15:27).

The problem began with the conversion of Constantine after the Battle of the Milvian Bridge in 312. How deeply Christian the Emperor was is a disputed and controversial point which need not occupy us here. Enough to say that Christianity became part of the establishment (a doubtful blessing indeed) with a growing sense of its duty to defend the Empire. We find Augustine (354–430) urging the soldier Boniface not to retire to a monastery but to take up arms in defense of the North African cities menaced by barbarian hordes. The same Augustine elaborated the "just war" theory which dominated Catholic moral theology until the Second Vatican Council. In fairness to Augustine we must remember that he wrote at a time when Rome was on the verge of collapse (it fell ignominiously in 411 before the onslaught of Alaric the Goth) and the barbarians were at the gates of Hippo where he was bishop.

I need not here trace the history of the just war theory. Only let me say that the mystical approach of the fathers gave way to the casuistic, legalistic approach of moral theologians with their endless distinctions and quibbles about when one may or may not kill. In the last chapter I said that love for the Lady Poverty was replaced by a collection of rules about poverty. Now let me add that love for the Prince of Peace was replaced by a collection of casuistic rules about when it was licit to make war, to kill, and to destroy. It is one more example of the awful wound inflicted on Christianity by the weakening of its mystical life.

## VI

Yet the Holy Spirit is always at work; and I see developing in our poor world a new spirituality, a vibrant and beautiful spirituality of peace. It has been germinating for decades; it will bring forth more luxuriant fruit as time goes on. Ecumenical in nature, this spirituality is associated with the names of Mahatma Gandhi, Martin Luther King, Jr., Thomas Merton, Dorothy Day, Mother Teresa, Helder Camara, Daniel Berrigan, and a host of others. It takes its inspiration from the gospel but is open to the influence of non-Christian religions. It is greatly inspired by *Pacem in Terris* of Pope John, by *Populorum Progressio* of Pope Paul, by numerous statements of the World Council of Churches, by statements of the Latin American bishops. This spiritual current influenced the whole Jesuit order which in 1975 made a radical commitment to justice and peace as well as to solidarity with the poor.

This is a real mysticism for our time. I call it mysticism because it demands a total commitment to justice and nonviolence far beyond anything that reason could ask for. It is for people who are so much in love with peace and the Prince of Peace that they are willing to sell everything for the field in which the treasure lies buried. It is for people who glory in the cross of Our Lord Jesus Christ. Gandhi said powerfully that the violent person knows how to kill but the nonviolent person knows how to die. Indeed, anyone who makes a commitment to this way must be prepared to suffer and to die as did Gandhi, as did Martin Luther King, Jr., as did Anwar Sadat, as did Archbishop Romero. For the path to peace is drenched in blood: it is a path of martyrdom. Hence the shocking paradox that Jesus does not bring peace but the sword.

Let me outline some of the characteristics of this mystical

movement, remembering that the process is still in its infancy and will grow to maturity as the years pass by.

1. It is a spirituality of total dedication to the poor. Not to the poor in a merely humanitarian sense but to the poor in whom one finds God. Listen to Gandhi:

> I count no sacrifice too great for the sake of seeing God face to face. The whole of my activity whether it may be called social, political, humanitarian or ethical is directed to that end. And as I know that God is found more often in the lowliest of His creatures than in the high and mighty I am struggling to reach the status of these. I cannot do so without their service. Hence my passion for the service of the suppressed classes.

In these words we find not only great compassion but also great faith. Gandhi himself said that he embraced nonviolence not because it was a successful way of liberating India from British rule but because it was the right thing to do. Its aim was not just freedom for the people but also the conversion of the oppressor. Gandhi had great faith in God, great faith in the power of truth.

2. It is a spirituality of radical nonviolence which refuses to tolerate killing of any kind even as a last resort, even in defensive action. It believes that there is no alternative to peace and that violence is no longer a way of solving problems. Hence it opposes both institutionalized violence and terrorist violence, leaving its adherents in a position of total vulnerability. It is a spirituality of forgiveness of one's enemy, of turning the other cheek, of giving one's coat as well as one's cloak.

But here let me be clear. It is not a spirituality of ignominious surrender. Rather does it explore just anger, channelling human energy into righteous indignation and passionate love for justice. It fights by nonfighting, by suffering, by witnessing to the truth, by defying unjust authority. It demands not only great courage but also great intelligence—lovers of peace find ingenious ways of expressing their dissent in nonviolent ways. And they are willing to dialogue with the adversary, always courteous, always simple like the dove, always wise like the serpent.

3. It is a way of life. For it is one thing to undergo a conversion: it is another thing to live out this conversion in daily life. This spirituality demands a change of life-style whereby a love for peace and for the poor pervade one's every action and operate in all one's relationships. It is not enough to demonstrate against nuclear weapons (good and laudable though this is), we must also change our way of thinking and our way of living.

4. It believes that one best helps the poor by education—by raising their consciousness, by giving them a sense of their human dignity. Pope Paul said well that "the new name for peace is development." He spoke of "integral human development" meaning education of the whole person, including that person's religious and spiritual qualities.

"Wonderful," you say. "But you are talking activism, not mysticism. Where is the mystical element in all this frenetic work for peace and social justice?"

I'm glad you mentioned that. The task confronting us today is to unite activism with mysticism. And the spiritual movement I here describe tries to do just that. You ask for the mystical element?

First, all mysticism is summed up in the *Fiat* of Mary. Let it be done. Let God act. Let the forces of the universe work. *Wu-wei*. And this spirituality leaves everything to God. It believes in the power of truth, the power of the cross, the power of suffering, the power of death, the power of all those seemingly negative things which make way for the action of God and are finally the most positive of all. What could be more mystical than this?

Again, looked at rationally this spirituality is crazy, as the cross is crazy. The more reasonable policy might be to build up nuclear weapons, to defend oneself, to liquidate the enemy. Many stolid Christians take this position. They talk as though Jesus Christ was the great proponent of common sense. How little they understand the gospel! How little they understand the cross! "We preach Christ crucified, a stumbling block to Jews and folly to Gentiles, but to those who are called, both Jews and Greeks, Christ the power of God and the wisdom of God" (1 Corinthians 1:23–24). The foolishness of the cross is at the center of the Christian mystical experience.

Can we dare hope that people of goodwill throughout the world will unite in this spirituality of peace? Can we hope that mystical and prophetic leaders will give us the guidance we need? Can we hope that the great religions, transcending sectarianism, will teach their disciples to love and to work for peace and justice? Listen to one great prophet of peace. Speaking to young people in France in 1981 Archbishop Helder Camara said:

> Shake the world. . . . You young people, bursting with intelligence and creative imagination, prepare exhibitions and shows to demonstrate the folly of the arms race and to show what could be done with this money if it were to be spent otherwise. . . . Political and military forces spend a million dollars per minute, $640 billion per year, to prepare for war and to manufacture nuclear arms. . . . We know today that a nuclear submarine can carry 20 missiles which can destroy 800 cities like Hiroshima and Nagasaki. . . . Is it not frightening? This could provoke a nuclear war capable of destroying all life on earth. . . . Bread should be shared among all. Last year 50 million people died of hunger and the United Nations says that two-thirds of the world's population lives in subhuman conditions. . . . We must go to the root of the problem,

we must go to justice. . . . Avoid the scandal of a small group
of countries always richer because they crush the others,
crush nearly all humanity. . . . Be people determined to create a more livable world.

The power of the masses is immense. Public opinion can stop
wars and halt the arms race. Tyrannical governments fear nonviolence much more than terrorism. Religion, an updated religion, can be an irresistible force in our modern world.

### VII

"Beautiful!" you say. "But I have one more problem.
You started this book with a promise to show me the unique and
distinctive dimension of Christian mysticism, and you end up
with Gandhi, with a Buddhist temple on the Mount of Olives—
just as earlier you glorified Buddhist poverty, quoted Albert Einstein and spoke about the koan and the mandala. How come?"

I hear you. Let me be frank. I did not foresee that I would
end this way. But as I wrote, the conviction grew within me
that Christians can no longer stand alone. If we are to be faithful to Jesus of Nazareth, if we are to be faithful to the gospel in
the modern world, if we are to be faithful to the Holy Spirit
acting in the Council and in the masses of the people, in short
if we are to be faithful to our vocation as Christians, we must
join hands with people of other faiths. We must humbly learn
from their theological insights and their age-old wisdom. We
must learn from them while sharing our own treasures. Together
with them we must work for a world peace which we alone
cannot construct.

So if we want mysticism, let us first get beyond narrow sectarianism to authentic Christianity. Our challenge is to cooperate with others while retaining our identity and allowing them
to retain theirs. Concretely, this means cooperating with others

while growing in love for Jesus Christ and the gospel. This is the way of the future.

NOTE

1. *Contra Celsum* C.5, 33.

# 15

# The Irish
# Conflict

I

I was born in the Falls Road, Belfast, in 1925. A few years before my birth, Ireland had been partitioned by the Tory government in Westminster so that the six northern counties fell under the control of the Protestant government in Stormont. The Falls Road was the heart of the Catholic ghetto and I knew from the beginning that I belonged to a persecuted and despised minority. Catholics were called papists or croppies or taigues. "Croppy, lie down!" was the order. But the croppies in the Falls did not lie down, and the Falls was proud of its fighting spirit. We called it the fearless, fervent, fighting Falls.

Some years before I was born my parents lived in a Protestant part of Belfast, but sectarian violence was so extreme that they exchanged houses with a Protestant who lived in the Catholic Falls and wanted to get out. My childhood was filled with stories of the revolution of 1916 but more especially of the violence that racked Belfast in the early 1920s. My parents were not violent people but they did sympathize with the republican movement, and the I.R.A. gunmen took shelter in our house.

We were sometimes raided by the military. My mother had to take the babies out of bed while the British soldiers stuck bayonets in the mattress looking for guns. When they came banging on the door in the early hours of the morning she had to answer. If my father went to the door the soldiers might shoot on sight: more than one father of a family had fallen dead in a pool of blood in his own hallway. Besides, we heard the story of the MacMahons. The British soldiers had taken MacMahon and his five sons down to the parlor and shot them dead in the presence of their mother. And then that terrifying pogrom at the bottom of the Falls, where families were burnt out of their houses, brutally terrorized, and left homeless.

But the struggle went on. The caged armored cars rumbled down the Falls and from within the I.R.A. prisoners sang:

> O wrap the green flag round me, boys,
> To die were far more sweet
> With Erin's noble emblem, boys,
> To be my winding-sheet.

The melody was beautiful and haunting. The men who sang it were idealists willing and happy to lay down their lives for Ireland. Moreover, they were religious people. My father had a picture of a uniformed Irish soldier sitting in a dimly lit cell, rosary in hand, and underneath was the caption:

> Blessed are they who suffer persecution for justice' sake; for theirs is the kingdom of heaven. [Matthew 5:10]

The picture remained in a drawer. It might have been dangerous to hang it on the wall.

My father told me of how from the window he once watched "the Protestant crowd" returning from a funeral. As they passed in front of our house some of them, a litle tipsy, began to dance in the middle of the road and to sing a famous anti-papist song:

"O Dolly's braes . . . we'll kick the Pope right over Dolly's braes." And then quite suddenly, three shots rang out and three of them fell dead on the street. The rest fled like frightened animals. That was the fearless, fervent, fighting Falls.

When I was still young my family moved to Liverpool. But we always returned to the North for holidays. I remember lying beside my brother in bed in my grandfather's house in Larne, listening to the muffled Orange drums in the distance. The drummers, we heard, boasted of beating those drums until blood poured from their wrists. During the day we sometimes watched the Orange processions. Row upon row of bowler hats, grim red faces, black suits, orange sashes. The drums, the flutes, the big banners of King Billy crossing the Boyne on his white horse. And the message was: "No surrender. No surrender. No surrender. No surrender. Not an inch. No pope here! Croppy, lie down!" We trembled with fear.

I have spoken here of "Protestant" and "Catholic" because that is the terminology with which I grew up. But, of course, Lloyd George had no interest in religion when he partitioned the country. What mattered was that the so-called Protestants were loyalists and the so-called Catholics were republicans. And that is one of the saddest aspects of the Irish conflict. Religion was unscrupulously used for political ends. Religion was shamelessly tied to ideology and culture. It became axiomatic that to be a good Protestant one must fanatically wave the Union Jack and to be a good Catholic one must reverently salute the Tricolor. Of course this is a distortion of the gospel. Yet it continues today. The challenge confronting Christians of all denominations is to liberate themselves from ideologies to discover anew the true meaning of the gospel of Jesus Christ, to find their identity as Christians. To this I shall return.

## II

To understand the Irish situation today one must go back in history to the eighteenth century. Then Ireland, once the island of saints and scholars, Ireland which had seen a wonderful flourishing of monasticism, Ireland which had sent missionaries to all parts of Europe lay broken and bleeding, exploited, improverished, and destroyed.

In response to the oppression, two traditions arose, one violent and the other nonviolent.

The outstanding prophet of nonviolence (and in my opinion the greatest of the Irish prophets) was Daniel O'Connell (1775–1847). Known in Ireland as "the liberator," O'Connell came from a well-to-do Irish family, was educated in France, and studied law in London. A brilliant orator, he had great respect for the law, a great love for the common people, a strong dislike for violence of any kind, a great love for peace. He had seen the violent uprising of 1798. He had witnessed the hangings, the flogging, the pitch-capping, the unspeakable cruelty; and he was determined to liberate the people "by peaceable, legal and constitutional means *and by none other.*"[1]

His first great victory was Catholic Emancipation. According to the penal laws, Catholics in both England and Ireland were not allowed to sit in parliament. In 1828 O'Connell contested a by-election in Clare, won an overwhelming majority and forced the British government to pass the Emancipation Act permitting Catholics to take their place in the House of Commons. With this, O'Connell became a popular hero, celebrated in song and in story. "O'Connell's in for Clare and all the bells are ringing" ran a popular ballad. People, priests, bishops—all were enthusiastically on his side.

His next objective was self-government for Ireland and a repeal of the Act of Union whereby the two countries had become one. O'Connell formed a political association for the masses of the people, who paid a penny a month. He held monster meetings, the greatest of which took place on August 15, 1843, on the royal hill of Tara where about a million people assembled—O'Connell's stentorian voice being carried from row to row so that everyone heard his message. But when another monster meeting was planned for Clontarf, the British government became alarmed and banned it. O'Connell, always committed to peace and seeing that rioting and massacres could take place, ordered the people to go home. Directed by his lieutenants, the great crowd dispersed quietly. No monster meeting took place. A week later O'Connell was arrested for conspiracy. He died at Lyons on May 15, 1847, commending his body to Ireland, his heart to Rome, and his soul to God.

I have sketched the career of O'Connell in the briefest terms. What I really want to say is that he is a prophet for our day; for he points to that conversion of heart which is the key to peace in the twentieth century. I do not say he was a saint. I do not propose him as a candidate for Catholic canonization. Irish men and women are well aware of his human weaknesses. Neither do I say that his policies of the nineteenth century should be followed literally in the twentieth. What I say is that he points to conversion in four crucial areas.

1. O'Connell was totally committed to peace and justice. He had a great abhorrence of bloodshed and a passion for solving problems by what we now call dialogue. His famous phrase (authentic or not I do not know) that *the freedom of Ireland was not worth the shedding of one drop of human blood* was quoted against him as Ireland became increasingly violent. So also was his statement that human blood *is no cement for the temple of liberty.* Men of violence quoted these words as proof that O'Connell did not care about liberty. Yet O'Connell had the courage to go to prison, referring to himself as "one who would give the last drop

of his life's blood and smile to see it flow to do any good for Ireland."[2]

2. He was totally committed to the people, whom he loved and served. Indeed, it was precisely his love for the people that hastened his death. Famine had come to Ireland, and in his last speech a broken and prematurely aged O'Connell pleaded with the House of Commons: "Ireland is in your hands. If you do not save her, she cannot save herself. I solemnly call on you to recollect that I predict with the greatest conviction that one-fourth of her population will perish unless you come to her relief."[3] In fact one-eighth of the population died; one-eighth crossed the Atlantic to the United States; and Ireland's population of eight million was almost halved in twenty years.

3. He wanted to weld Irish men and women of all religious denominations into one community. "In the struggle for nationality I recognize no distinction of creed or party. Every man who joins with me for Ireland is my sworn brother."[4] And again: "The Protestant alone could not expect to liberate his country— the Roman Catholic alone could not do it—neither the Presbyterian—but amalgamate the three into one Irishman, and the union (between England and Ireland) is defeated."[5]

4. He had a great love for Britain and for the British monarchy. Not that he was blind to the cruel injustice of British rule; but he saw sincere and friendly cooperation between the two countries as the only path to peace and prosperity.

Such was O'Connell. And the nonviolent tradition continued after his death. The parliamentarians or constitutionalists, as his followers were called, excogitated ingenious ways of peaceful opposition. They invented the boycott which takes its name from the English landlord against whom they fought. Then there were the obstructionists who made long speeches in the House of Commons and bored their adversaries to death. Nonviolent patriots arose, the greatest of whom was the Protestant landlord Charles Stewart Parnell. In short, a peaceful yet powerful movement for Irish liberty surged on.

And the spirit of O'Connell is alive in Ireland today. It lives in O'Connell Street in Dublin. It lives in some able politicians in the North who seek the welfare of the people in constitutional and peaceful ways. I believe that the salvation of Ireland (and perhaps of England too) depends upon a resurgence of the nonviolence of O'Connell.

For I like to think of him as the Gandhi of Ireland. Like Gandhi he was in love with peace and nonviolence; like Gandhi he loved the poor and has been called "the king of the beggars"; like Gandhi he was a profoundly religious person who had flagrant defects; like Gandhi he died broken and disappointed; like Gandhi his greatest influence was after his death. Yes, O'Connell speaks to the world today, and only by following his principles can we have peace in Ireland or elsewhere.

But side by side with the nonviolence of O'Connell was another movement, a violent movement. This also was quasi-religious. It developed into a mysticism of blood, a mysticism of the gun, a mysticism of death and killing. This also, alas, is alive in Ireland today as it was all around me in my childhood. O'Connell saw its rise and he warned the British people that if justice was not done to Ireland there would be "bloody revolution and separation between the two countries."[6] About this mysticism of violence let me now say a word.

### III

The Irish idealization of violence stems from the French Revolution and in particular from one of the great Irish patriots of that time: Theobald Wolfe Tone (1763–98). A Dublin-born Protestant, Tone was at first ambitious to do great things for England; but, rebuffed by the British government, his love turned to hate. He joined the Society of United Irishmen founded mainly by Presbyterians in Belfast and committed to the establishment of an Irish Republic. His great ideal now was "to break the connection with England, the never-failing source of all our political evil."[7] While love for liberty and love for Ireland were strong in his heart it is undeniable that he was consumed by hatred. "The truth is," he writes in his autobiography, "I hate the very name of England; I hated her before my exile; I hate her since; and I will hate her always."[8] And elsewhere he asserts: "I was led by a hatred of England so deeply rooted in my nature that it was rather an instinct than a principle."[9]

Arrested and condemned to death for treason in collaborating with the French, Tone cut his own throat with a penknife to escape the humiliation of the gallows. But his spirit lived on. His hatred, it is true, was modified. Subsequent patriots distinguished classically between hating the sin and hating the sinner. But Tone's ideal of a Republic of Ireland separated from England and his conviction that this could only be achieved through violence and armed insurrection—this lived on in the hearts of a series of heroic patriots who died on the gallows for the freedom of their country. The most famous and romantic of these was Robert Emmett (1778–1803) who became a myth and a legend:

> Bold Robert Emmett, the darling of Erin
> Bold Robert Emmett, he died with a smile:
> Farewell my companions both loyal and daring
> I lay down my life for the Emerald Isle

Emmett believed in violence. He challenged the British Empire. And he died a martyr's death. His "speech from the dock" is one of the great documents of Irish revolutionary literature.

Yet the violent movement never won the hearts of the masses as did the movement of O'Connell. It did not win the support of clergy and bishops. It never became a popular movement—

until 1916 when it produced a whole literature of drama and poetry and song, when it became associated with the revival of the Irish language, when it became profoundly religious. The "Rising" took place in Easter week and the patriots believed that as Jesus died and rose so they would die and their spirits would rise in a liberated and glorified Ireland.

And so, in the poetic words of W. B. Yeats, "a terrible beauty was born." It was terrible because of the blood, Irish blood and English blood, that was destined to flow. It was terrible because of the hatred, the fear, and craving for revenge, the guilt, the remorse, and the psychological agony that it brought. Yet it was beautiful too—full of heroism, idealism, selfless dedication, sacrifice, and love of country; it was beautiful, too, in the inspiration it gave to anticolonial struggles throughout the world. The most representative spokesman of this terrible beauty was Patrick Pearse (1879–1916) about whom a few words may be in place.

Born in Dublin of an English father and an Irish mother, Pearse was a poet, an educator, a prophet. He devoted himself to the study of the Celtic language and of ancient Irish literature. Above all he was mesmerized by Wolfe Tone claiming that "God spoke to Ireland through Tone." Listen to his words at the grave of Tone in Bodenstown in 1913:

> We have come to the holiest place in Ireland; holier to us even than the place where Patrick sleeps in Down. Patrick brought us life, but this man died for us. . . . He was the greatest of Irish Nationalists; I believe he was the greatest of Irish men. And if I am right in this I am right in saying that we stand in the holiest place in Ireland, for it must be that the holiest sod of a nation's soil is the sod where the greatest of her dead lies buried.[10]

For Pearse holiness is equated with fanatical love for Ireland leading to the supreme sacrifice.

As time went on he became increasingly preoccupied with the sanctity of bloodshed and the nobility of death. In December 1915 he writes of the war in Europe:

> The last sixteen months have been the most glorious in the history of Europe. Heroism has come back to the earth. . . . It is good for the world that such things should be done. The old heart of the earth needed to be warmed with the red wine of the battlefields. Such august homage was never offered to God as this, the homage of millions of lives given gladly for love of country. . . .[1]

And to this he adds that "Ireland has not known the exhilaration of war for a hundred years." But bloodshed must come to Ireland:

> We must accustom ourselves to the thought of arms, to the sight of arms, to the use of arms. We may make mistakes in the beginning and shoot the wrong people; but bloodshed is a cleansing and a sanctifying thing, and the nation which regards it as the final horror has lost its manhood. There are many things more horrible than bloodshed; and slavery is one of them.[12]

These are the words of a dreamer as Frank Shaw well understands when he astutely observes that Pearse "wrote fiery words about shooting people; but he did not himself use any weapon; and we would be surprised if he had."[13] He certainly never foresaw where his words were leading. If he had seen the cruel civil war of 1922, would he have said that bloodshed is a cleansing thing? If he had seen the murder in the streets of Belfast in 1983, would he have said that bloodshed is a sanctifying thing? Or what would he have said and thought?

Pearse was commander-in-chief of the Irish forces in the Rising. On April 30 he sent out an order to his troops to surrender. He himself was arrested and executed at 3:30 A.M. on May 3,

1916. Shortly before his death he wrote to his mother: "I have just received Holy Communion. I am happy except for the great grief of parting from you. This is the death I should have asked for if God had given me the choice of all deaths—to die a soldier's death for Ireland and for freedom."[14] At the same time, through a Capuchin priest, he gave to his mother a poem about Mary, the mother of Jesus, who offered her firstborn son to the Father.

Yet another influential figure in the mysticism of blood is Terence McSweeney, a member of the I.R.A., who died at Brixton in October 1920 after seventy-four days on hunger strike. In his inaugural speech as Lord Mayor of Cork McSweeney had said:

> The contest on our side is not one of rivalry or vengeance, but of endurance. It is not those who can inflict the most, but those who suffer the most who will conquer.[15]

These words, profoundly mystical, are far from Wolfe Tone. They express Christian belief in the power of suffering, in the power of Christ's cross. They are the Christian version of the Taoist *wu-wei* and they remind us of Gandhi's belief in the victory of suffering. They were quoted by the I.R.A. hunger strikers when they began their fast-to-death in the Maze prison in 1980.

And so the terrible beauty was born; and it is still alive. It is alive in the Republic where politician, priest, and prelate stand to attention for the national anthem, *The Soldier's Song*, singing "Soldiers are we . . . impatient for the coming fight . . . mid cannon's roar and rifle's peal we'll chant a soldier's song." But it is even more alive in the North. Mass media in Britain have depicted the I.R.A. as thugs and hooligans and gangsters. In fact many of them are idealistic and intelligent people imbued with the philosophy of Patrick Pearse. Many of them are profoundly religious. They look on themselves as soldiers fighting for the liberation of their country and completing the unfinished business of 1916. They have their own moral theology and consider their bombing campaign a good deal more moral than that of people who annihilated thousands of innocent people in Dresden and Dusseldorf and the other German cities. They claim that their violence is a *last resort*, that the British government has again and again made promises which it does not keep and does not intend to keep, that one cannot trust Britain, that the only way to look at the Brits is down the barrel of a gun.

I myself do not agree with this nor do I accept the "last resort" theory as a justification for war. All I am saying here is that many of the I.R.A. are sincere people—the hunger strike proved their sincerity and their willingness to die. Listen to Father Denis Faul, chaplain to the Maze prison, speaking about Bobby Sands who died on May 5, 1980, after sixty-six days on hunger strike;

> Sands himself said to me: 'Greater love than this hath no man.' He himself had been beaten, and he'd heard young prisoners screaming every night as they were tortured and beaten by the officers. And Sands said: 'I will put a stop to this.' He laid his own life on the line. He was a very noble man, and his sacrifice was a very noble sacrifice, and the whole world responded to it.[15]

The world did indeed respond.

## IV

In evaluating the Irish violence of 1916 and the religious patriotism of Pearse, we must never forget the context. This was the time of the First World War when English poets like Rupert Brooke were singing idealistically about death and glory. It was the time when Christian clergymen were ranting and raving about the beauty of killing the enemy. Listen to the words of the Anglican Bishop of London in 1915:

> ... to save the freedom of the world, everyone who loves freedom and honour, everyone who puts principle before ease and life before mere living, is banded in a great crusade—we cannot deny it—to kill Germans, to kill them not for the sake of killing, but to save the world, to kill the young as well as the old, to kill those who have shown kindness to our wounded as well as those who crucified the Canadian soldier, who sank the Lusitania, and who turned the machine guns on the civilians of Aerschot and Louvain; and to kill them lest civilization itself be killed.[16]

When we reflect that this sermon is typical of a hundred others, when we reflect that theologians were busy justifying mass slaughter with their little principle of double effect, Pearse's talk about the cleansing and sanctifying power of blood sounds less shocking.

And yet, taking these mitigating circumstances into account, *what can we say except that Pearse was a false mystic and that his doctrine has brought untold suffering to Ireland?* Let me say what I mean by false mysticism.

Christian mysticism, as I have tried to say in this book, is a total commitment to God expressing itself in an unconditional, unrestricted love that goes on and on, leading to altered states of consciousness and new levels of awareness. The great challenge for the mystic is to keep that love unconditional and unrestricted (that is to say, not to let it be conditioned or restricted by any object less than God) and not to be sidetracked by any idol. Hence St. John of the Cross' *nada, nada, nada:* nothing, nothing, nothing.

Now Pearse seems to have had a total commitment and a great love. Artistic by nature he may also have enjoyed altered states of consciousness and new levels of awareness. But his love became restricted: the object of his love and commitment became Ireland. The liberty of Ireland was his idol. He confused patriotism with holiness—this is clear from his speech at the grave of Wolfe Tone which I have quoted. In 1915 he composed a short Christmas poem to Jesus Christ:

> O King that was born
> To set bondsmen free,
> In the coming battle,
> Help the Gael![17]

Here Pearse insinuates that Jesus was born to liberate Ireland from British oppression. Frank Shaw rightly observes that this is a misinterpretation of the gospel. "Christ," he writes, "was not born to set bondsmen free from any chains other than those of sin. In the Judea of his day, Christ was set down in a situation comparable to that of Ireland in 1916. Christ made it unmistakably plain that he was not a national savior, and his words to his disciples on the day of the Ascension expressed his sorrow that those who knew him and who loved him could continue so long in error."[18]

Traditionally one judges mystical experience by its fruits. The fruit of the spirit, writes St. Paul, is "love, joy, peace, patience, kindness, goodness, faithfulness, gentleness, self-control; against such there is no law" (Galatians 5:22). Now even the most ardent admirer of Pearse cannot say that this glorification of blood and death has brought love, joy, peace and patience to Ireland or to England. If one reflects on the horrors of the civil war of 1922–23 when, after killing the British invaders, Irishmen killed one another in the streets of Dublin and throughout the countryside; if one reflects on how members of the same family bitterly fought one another; if one goes further and sees the ruthless assassinations and the bloody campaign of the I.R.A. in the dancehalls and pubs of Belfast and Birmingham and London—then one looks in vain for the love, the joy, the peace, the patience of Paul.

However, when I say that Pearse was a false mystic I do not mean that he was an evil person. Far from it. He was profoundly heroic. And the people who sincerely live his ideology are also profoundly heroic. But they are also profoundly misguided. Their very sincerity and dedication makes them more dangerous than the blatant evildoer. They have brought unspeakable suffering to the very people they claimed to liberate.

## V

I have spoken about the oppression of the British government, about the nonviolent response of O'Connell and the violent response of Tone and Pearse. It remains to say something about the violence of the Orange Order in Ulster.

I need not go back in history to the conflict between the Catholic King James II and the Protestant King William of Orange. I need not go back in history to describe how Britain encouraged Protestants to settle in Ireland in order to secure the island against invasion by Catholic European powers. Enough to say that in 1795 the Orange Society was founded, taking its name from William of Orange. It quickly became violently anti-Catholic and was used adroitly by the Tory government in Britain. When William Gladstone introduced a bill to give Ireland home rule in 1886, Lord Randolf Churchill, father of Winston, made the famous or infamous remark that "the orange card is the one to play."[19] In short, he wanted to use the Orangemen against the home rulers. The same Churchill was willing and eager to stir up civil war for his own ends. "Ulster will fight and Ulster will be right," he cried—and Ulster prepared to fight.[20]

And the fighting spirit of Protestant Ulster had a religious dimension. "We will fight," declared one Presbyterian minister, "as men alone can fight who have the Bible in one hand and the sword in the other . . . and this will be our dying cry, echoed and re-echoed from earth to heaven and from one end of Ulster to the other: 'No Popery, no Surrender!' "[21]

"No Popery, no Surrender! No Pope here! Not an inch!" These are the slogans that have echoed through a century of Ulster's history. These are the slogans I heard as a child. These are the slogans painted large in the streets of Belfast today. Together with them goes a whole antipapist culture with parades and songs and dances. A July Twelfth song runs as follows:

> If guns are made for shooting,
> Then skulls were made to crack.
> You've never seen a better Taigue
> Than with a bullet in his back.

On September 28, 1913 nearly a quarter of a million Ulstermen signed a biblical document known as the *Solemn League and Covenant* to resist Home Rule—some of them signed it in their blood. This was followed by the formation of an Ulster Volunteer Force of 100,000 Protestant men recruited through the Orange Lodges.

And so in 1916 the Rising took place and in 1922 Ireland was partitioned. The six counties became an explicitly Protestant state with its parliament at Stormont.

The next sixty years are a record of criminal injustice on the part of Stormont and Westminster, and of criminal indifference on the part of Dublin. The Ulster Parliament was unashamedly "a protestant government for a protestant people." In 1933 Basil Brooke, later to become Prime Minister, voiced the sentiments of the establishment when he told loyalists "whenever possible to employ good protestant lads and lassies." In the *Londonderry*

*Sentinel* in March 1934 he said: "I recommend those people who are loyalists not to employ Roman Catholics, 99 percent of whom are disloyal. . . . If you don't act properly now, before we know where we are we shall find ourselves in a minority instead of a majority."

Needless to say, this was a blatant distortion of the words "Protestant" and "Catholic," which sincere Christians of any denomination would at once reject. But the Stormont Government, fearing that the republicans would outbreed the loyalists, believed that it could best stir up fanaticism by using religious terms and appealing to pseudoreligious sentiments. This religious terminology was encouraged by Westminster and tolerated by Dublin. It was unconsciously accepted by people in the North. It was the only terminology I knew.

And so Westminster kept remote control of the North by a draconian system of discrimination based on religious beliefs. In housing, in employment, in voting, Catholics were second-class citizens: they were frequently forced to leave the country because there was no work at home. And in this way (and with a blatant system of gerrymandering) Stormont retained its power.

Even worse than the discrimination was the police system. The *Special Powers Act* giving the Northern Ireland Minister of Home Affairs unlimited power to restrict liberty, to outlaw organizations, to detain people without charge or trial, to impose curfew, to restrict movements, to order arrests, to search without warrant—this became law in 1922 and was renewed annually until 1933 when it was made permanent. The North became a police state. I recall as an adolescent hearing how prisoners were flogged with "the cat." And how we dreaded seeing the infamous militia, the "B Specials," on those lonely roads in the glens of Antrim!

In the late sixties the frustration of the young was reaching breaking point. Dublin, with an unbelievable lack of courage, had made no attempt to draw world attention to the flagrant injustice in the six northern counties. And so a peaceful but determined civil-rights movement began. This was met with violent opposition by the Protestant majority, by the police, and by the British army, and with callous indifference by Dublin. A peaceful march from Belfast to Derry was ruthlessly attacked by Protestant terrorists while the police, there to give protection, turned tail and fled. At a public demonstration on January 30, 1972, now known as Bloody Sunday, the British army shot and killed thirteen civilians. Catholics were burned out of their houses in the lower Falls. As time went on things got worse and worse, with the British army terrorizing the civilian population. Listen to Father Faul about the situation during the hunger strike:

> The British army went out and behaved disgracefully, blew the heads of schoolgirls with plastic bullets: Carol Ann Kelly and Julie Livingstone. . . . They undoubtedly got a free hand to go into Catholic areas to beat, to maim, to kill, to do anything they liked to break the people. Absolute *carte blanche.*"[22]

Brutally terrorized by the army and the police, callously neglected by Dublin, is it surprising if some Catholics turned to the I.R.A.—not because they approved of the ruthless bombing and the savage assassinations, but because they had no other source of protection?

I need not here speak in detail about the tragic and horrifying war between the British army and the I.R.A. Irish men and women everywhere have surely been shocked and ashamed by the brutal murders committed by their fellow countryfolk. Equally shocking are the underground assassinations by the British army and the police as well as the fierce reprisals of the Protestant paramilitary groups. But worst of all are the accounts of torture.

Britain had borrowed "the five techniques" of interrogation from the Russian K.G.B. and used them in her colonial wars after 1946. Now these same techniques were used ruthlessly in Ireland, earning condemnation in two reports of Amnesty International (1972 and 1978) and damning decisions of the European Court of Human Rights and the European Commission of Human Rights in Strasbourg. The British government paid over a million pounds in damages, but this was little compensation for the punishment cells, the kicking, the beating, the prolonged standing, the deprivation of food and sleep.[23] Nor did it compensate for the trials without jury, the forced confessions, the threats, the prolonged psychological torture. Says Father Faul: "Men get thirty-year sentences for things of which they are legally innocent and really innocent."[24]

In 1973 a great effort towards a just solution was made at Sunningdale in Berkshire where London, Belfast, and Dublin got together to formalize power sharing in the North. But this was stymied by a massive strike organized by Protestant extremists. The failure of Sunningdale was indeed a dark hour for Ulster.

## V

I hear you say: "If O'Connell really won the hearts of the people, if the masses were really nonviolent, if the violent men were a tiny elite, how do you explain the spread of violence throughout the country?"

Violence spread because of the foolish intransigence of the British government. The masses of the people had little sympathy with the 1916 rising; some 90,000 Irishmen had joined the British army and were fighting side by side with Englishmen on the continent; but when General Maxwell ordered the execution of Pearse and his companions and when ninety-seven others were condemned to death, the whole people rose in righteous indignation. And after that the British government committed blunder upon blunder. The same is true in the North today. I smiled when I read the comments of Sean McBride, Nobel Peace Prize winner, whose father was executed with Pearse in 1916. Speaking to an American magazine about Northern Ireland today, McBride said: "I should have known from previous experience that when it comes to dealing with Ireland the British government and establishment lose all common sense and all sense of justice. . . . In their own country and in countries they do not seek to dominate, the British are reasonable, fair-minded and even lovable people. . . . In regard to Ireland, the British government and establishment are just *incapable* of being objective. . . . Fair-mindedness or justice does not exist."[25] Most Irish men and women who have lived abroad will resonate with McBride's remarks.

Even more severe is Desmond Wilson, a priest who lives in the heart of a Catholic ghetto in Belfast. Speaking of the "evils of British rule in Ireland," Father Wilson writes:

> The British government continually misrepresents the situation in Ireland by pretending that Protestants and Catholics are at each others' throats and that their troops are in Ireland as peacemakers. Nothing could be further from the truth. The people of Northern Ireland have made continuous and courageous efforts to solve economic, cultural and religious problems. All during my lifetime they have been frustrated by the British government which has deliberately created enmity and hatred between them. This it has done by lies and misrepresentations of one side to the other. In recent times its agents have been guilty also of assassinations designed to raise ill-feeling between sections of our population.

"What the British are doing in Ireland," Father Wilson concludes, "is unjust, vicious, and degrading. It has been, and is now, a persecution which at this moment has no parallel in Europe."[26]

Alas, the British government (particularly the Tory government) has still to learn that the answer to Irish terrorism is not ingenious antiterrorist tactics and cruel methods of interrogation but justice for everyone. Human nature can only stomach so much injustice. A repressed people can reach breaking point. And bloody terrorism can follow. The history of Ireland teaches this lesson to the modern world.

## VI

"And when he drew near and saw the city he wept over it, saying, 'Would that even today you knew the things that make for peace!' " (Luke 19:41).

To the British army, to the I.R.A., to the Orange Order, to Westminster, to Dublin the gospel says: Change your hearts! "Unless you repent you will all likewise perish" (Luke 13:5). The message is metanoia, conversion, change of heart.

I hear you say: "Conversion of heart in 10 Downing Street? Conversion of heart in Dublin? Conversion of the I.R.A. and the Orange Lodge? Unrealistic! Naive! You're out of your mind!"

Yes, I suppose I am. St. Paul says that anyone who believes the gospel of Jesus Christ is a fool. And I am trying to say that this gospel alone contains the solution. Only through a radical commitment to the gospel on the part of a significant number of people on both sides of the border and on both sides of the Irish Sea will peace and justice be born. We need ten just men and women. I know it will not be easy. I know how deep the wounds are; I know what it will cost to forgive. I know there will be martyrs and scapegoats. I know that the ten just men and women will look like fools. I know that those who speak clearly for justice will suffer the fate of all prophets. I know that the way of peace is more demanding than the way of violence. But it is the only way.

I hear you say: "But how can this conversion of heart become a living reality? You cannot deny that the institutional churches, both Catholic and Protestant, have roundly condemned violence and have thundered against murder from their pulpits everywhere. And this has had no effect whatsoever. The violent people continue on their own sweet way, ignoring the anathemas of their pastors and encouraged by the silent and sympathetic support of thousands of their fellow Christians. And as for the perpetrators of institutionalized violence, anyone who tries to convert them should have his or her head examined."

I hear you. We must take a new approach. Earlier in this book I said that the role of the institutional churches is more and more to teach the gospel, to teach prayer, to teach the people to discern, and to make their own free decisions. Indeed we are in an age of authentic mystical prayer with its attentiveness to the movements of the Spirit; and I believe that thousands of people in Ireland are ready for mysticism. Even some of the violent people may be ready for mysticism—for the only answer to false mysticism is authentic mysticism.

Rather than laying down the law, perhaps the institutional churches can unite to teach Christian people to pray: to sit quietly in God's loving presence, to sit with their anger (about this I have spoken in an earlier chapter) and to channel their energy in creative and constructive nonviolent paths. Through quiet, contemplative prayer people will learn to open their hearts to the love of the Spirit, a love that will heal the terrible wounds inflicted over many decades. Again they will learn to let life flow into their prayer: the agonies and the sufferings as well as the joys. In prayer they will learn to make decisions, not in times of impulsive anger, but under the gentle guidance of the Holy Spirit. Only when their commitment to justice and peace is the outcome of enlightenment, of conversion, of mystical experience, will they move the mountains that need to be moved.

Let us learn to sit in God's presence until the gospel comes to life at those archetypal levels where mysticism reigns. If I have stressed one thing in this book it is that intellectual understanding of the gospels is not enough. *Mysticism means loving the gospel, living the gospel and allowing ourselves to be transformed by the gospel.* Let me again mention some areas where the gospel will transform Ireland today.

First, the gospel calls us to love the poor. "I was hungry and you gave me food . . ." (Matthew 25:35). The poor are the unemployed, the despised, the outcasts, the prisoners, the exploited, the oppressed, those who suffer discrimination of any kind. The poor are the bereaved, those who have lost husband or father or son, those who have been wounded, those who have been tortured. The first conversion of heart leads to love of the poor be they Catholic or Protestant, Irish or English, loyalist or republican, saint or sinner, friend or foe.

Second, the gospel calls to renunciation of violence, whether it be institutionalized violence or terrorist violence. The gospel today calls for a love of peace that goes far beyond the old "just war" theories to an irrational (or should I say suprarational? or foolish?) commitment to love one's enemies. About this I have spoken at length in the last chapter. Here only let me say that unilateral renunciation of violence is a tremendous risk that can only come from profound enlightenment and deep prayer.

And let me here pause to refer to another relevant sentence from the gospel that sums up the history of Ireland and the history of the world: "All who take the sword will perish by the sword" (Matthew 26:52). Asian religions say something similar when they speak of *karma*, meaning that violence will recoil not only on the violent but also on their children and on the very people they strive to help. "Daughters of Jerusalem, do not weep for me, but weep for yourselves and for your children" (Luke 23:28). The victims of terrorism and the victims of institutionalized violence shout back from the grave to their killers: "You are hurting yourselves more than you are hurting us; you are piling up suffering for your children and for your country; weep for yourselves and for your children." All who take the sword will perish by the sword. This is the law of karma. This the law of life. You do not win through violence. The last will be first and the first last. Surely this is an ominous warning not only to Ireland and England but to the superpowers in today's world. Yet we must not forget that bad karma is washed away through metanoia or conversion of heart.

Third, the gospel calls for ecumenism. "By this all men will know that you are my disciples, if you have love one for another" (John 13:35). Let me repeat that, if Christians in Ireland are to love one another, they must first be liberated from enslavement to ideology (whether to the Tricolor or to the Union Jack) to find their common identity in a united gospel commitment to charity, justice, and peace.

I said that conversion of heart cannot be imposed from outside: it must be the outcome of prayer. Clearly we need the prayer not only of those actively involved in work for justice but of the whole population. Most of all we need the prayer of thousands of silent contemplatives everywhere who feel the pain of Ireland in their life of solitude.

For if we look back at the unhappy history of these two islands during the past two centuries, it is difficult to escape the conclusion that more than ordinary evil has been at work. If we look at the hatred, the cruelty, the assassinations, the torture, the injustice; if we reflect that much of this evil has been perpetuated in the name of God; if we see how the gospel has been misunderstood and how the Bible has been thumped; if we reflect that underlying everything is a craving for money and a lust for power on the part of a few who have manipulated the many; then we see that we are face to face with something that can only be expelled through prayer and fasting.

For prayer sees the problem at its roots. It sees that the greatest evil is sin. It sees that sin deep within ourselves. It sees that the most pitiable people are the oppressors, the murderers, the torturers, the rich, the powerful, the violent. These are the people who are lost, perhaps eternally lost; while the poor are blessed. For the conversion of sinners the contemplative prays.

I am aware that good things are happening in England and Ireland. There have been many cases of heroic forgiveness, of total dedication to peace and justice. Christians of different denominations are praying together. Contemplatives are offering their lives to God. These are signs of the Spirit.

And yet our hope for Ireland and our hope for the world does not lie precisely in all this. It rests on the fact that God so loved the world as to give His only Son and the wounded stag has appeared on the hill.[27]

## NOTES

1. Words of Daniel O'Connell in a letter to the Bishop of Dromore. See Cecil Woodham-Smith, *The Great Hunter* (New York: Harper & Row, 1962), p. 104.
2. Robert Kee, *The Most Distressful Country* (London: Quartet Books, 1976), p. 203.
3. Ibid., p. 258.
4. Ibid., p. 180.
5. Ibid.
6. Ibid., p. 233.
7. See Francis Shaw, "The Canon of Irish History," *Studies*, Dublin, Summer 1972.
8. Ibid.
9. Ibid.
10. Ibid.

11. Ibid.
12. Ruth Dudley Edwards, *Patrick Pearse: The Triumph of Failure* (New York: Taplinger, 1978; London: Gollancz, 1977), p. 179.
13. Shaw, "The Canon of Irish History."
14. Edwards, *Patrick Pearse*, p. 322.
15. *National Catholic Reporter*, Kansas City, July 30, 1982.
16. Enda McDonagh, *Church and Politics* (South Bend: Univ. of Notre Dame Press, 1980), p. 62.
17. Patrick Pearse, *Plays, Stories, Poems* (Dublin: Helicon, 1980), p. 340.
18. Shaw, "The Canon of Irish History."
19. Robert Kee, *Ireland: A History* (Boston: Little, Brown, 1982; London: Weindenfeld & Nicholson, 1980), p. 140.
20. Ibid., p. 138.
21. Ibid.
22. *National Catholic Reporter*, Kansas City, July 30, 1982.
23. Ibid.
24. For more detailed information see Denis Faul and Raymond Murray, "H-Block and Its Background," *The Catholic Mind*, May 1981.
25. Janet Cassidy, "An Interview with Sean McBride," *The Sign*, November, 1981.
26. *National Catholic Reporter*, Kansas City, October 15, 1982.
27. For the theme of conversion in Ireland see the writings of Enda McDonagh and John Austin Baker in the Irish journal *The Furrow*.

# 16

# The
# Woman

I

This book has been an exploration into the roots of Christian mysticism, an attempt to see what is unique, special, and distinctive in the Christian mystical path. Such an effort, however, would be woefully incomplete without a chapter on the role of the Virgin Mary. For she is the star of the sea, enlightening weary travelers, guiding them sweetly through turbulent waters to the gate of heaven.

Before speaking about mysticism proper, however, let me say a word about the role of Mary in the ordinary Christian life.

II

Mary plays a central role in the Christian story, particularly in the story of redemption. It all begins with Genesis which is a man-woman story, a deeply human drama wherein Eve has a principal role, playing opposite Adam and cooperating in his sin. Where would Genesis be without Eve?

And as the Fall is a man-woman story, so the Redemption, in the interpretation of the church fathers, is also a man-woman story. It is the story of Jesus and Mary. Remember how Paul speaks of Jesus as the second Adam: "The first man was from the earth, a man of dust; the second man is from heaven" (1 Corinthians 15:47). And the church fathers, commenting on Paul, speak of Mary as the second Eve. "Comparing Mary with Eve, they call her 'the mother of the living,' and still more ofen they say: 'death through Eve, life through Mary.' "[1] Again, the fourth gospel sees Mary as "the woman" to whom Jesus entrusts the beloved disciple and the whole human family. And Christian tradition sees this beautiful woman looking across the centuries to the first woman with whom the human race began. In short, as Eve cooperated with Adam in the sin of the world, so Mary cooperates with Jesus in giving life to the same world.

In all this, however, the Council warns against exaggerations. "We have but one Mediator, as we know from the words of the Apostle. . . . For all the saving influences of the Blessed Virgin on men originate, not from some inner necessity, but from the divine pleasure."[2] And even more directly the Council states:

> The Church does not hesitate to profess this subordinate role of Mary. She experiences it continuously and commends it to the hearts of the faithful, so that encouraged by this maternal help they may more closely adhere to the Mediator and Redeemer.[3]

The subordinate role of Mary is something the Christian consciousness accepts quite naturally. It never seems that Mary is, so to speak, downgraded. For there is another kind of equality: an equality arising from love. Of this equality Jesus spoke when he called his disciples "friends." "No longer do I call you servants . . . but I have called you friends . . ." (John 15:14, 15). Here Jesus lovingly raises the disciples to the status of equals and his words were later concretized in the doctrine that, as

Jesus was son by nature, we are sons and daughters by grace. Now my point is that what is true of the disciples is preeminently true of Mary to whom Scripture and tradition ascribe a unique role in the drama of salvation. Some theologians have even spoken of her as coredemptrix.

About Mary's privileges I need not speak in detail. Scripture scholars find more and more wealth in the early chapters of the third gospel. Archaeologists find ample inscriptions witnessing to a primitive church praying fervently to Mary. The apocryphal writings of the second and third centuries show us Christians fascinated by the person of Mary. After the Council of Ephesus (431), love for Mary grows both in the cultured monastic life and in the hearts of the illiterate masses. In short, the whole church, people and shepherds alike, pour forth prayers to the Mother of God.

But to understand the Catholic approach to Mary, one must understand the Catholic aproach to scriptural interpretation, a point with which I have struggled throughout this book. The Council, speaking of the role of Mary in the Old Testament, writes: "These earliest documents, *as they are read in the Church and are understood in the light of a further and full revelation,* bring the figure of the woman, Mother of the Redeemer, into a gradually sharper focus."[4] I italicize these words to emphasize that the Council goes beyond the historical-critical approach to the fuller sense or *sensus plenior*. It finds references to Mary in Genesis, in Isaiah, in Micah, just as the Christian tradition has always found her in the wisdom literature.

What I am saying is that the praying church (the *ecclesia orans*) throughout the ages has well understood this equality stemming from love and from unique privilege. The praying people have well understood the love of Jesus for Mary and of Mary for Jesus. Forms of the Jesus prayer illustrates this well. There is, for example, the formula: "Jesus, Mary" or "Jesus,

Mary and Joseph" or again (a formula which brings out the paradox of subordination and equality) "Jesus mercy: Mary help." I need not speak here of the *Memorare* of Bernard of Clairvaux, of the *Salve Regina* chanted hauntingly each evening in the hushed atmosphere of Cistercian monasteries, of the rosary recited by millions throughout the world. Enough to say that in Catholic spirituality of the last few centuries intimacy with Jesus and Mary has found a special place, expressing itself symbolically in the Sacred Heart of Jesus and the Immaculate Heart of Mary. The two hearts are one. Love for Jesus and love for Mary are not two things, but one thing.

Coming to mysticism, let me recall my earlier thesis that Christian mysticism consists in living the Christian mystery and being transformed by it. Now I say that if we really live the mystery of Christ we will discover that we are also living the mystery of Mary. For she shares preeminently in the mystery of her Son. We will find that we are living the mystery of Jesus and Mary; we will find that we are transformed not only in the image of Jesus but also in the image of Mary.

### III

I hear you say: "I resonate with what you say and it sounds theologically palatable. But I still have questions. The Protestant reformers were part of the *ecclesia orans*; yet they rebelled against the special cult of Mary. Moreover, some modern Christians protest that devotion to Mary detracts from that commitment to Jesus which is the very center of the Christian life. What do you say to that?"

It is true that some modern Christians are not enthusiastic about devotion to Mary. But were the reformers like that? A Lutheran scholar, writing in *America* about the Virgin Mary, speaks of "the extraordinarily similar sentiments of the Father of the Reformation, Martin Luther, and of the Fathers of the Second Vatican Council."[5] In fact Luther had great devotion to Mary. He wrote copiously about her. He defended her perpetual virginity. He kept an image of the Virgin on the wall of his study. Listen to his prayer in his beautifully moving meditation on the *Magnificat*:

> O Blessed Virgin, Mother of God, you were nothing and all despised; yet God in His grace regarded you and worked such great things in you. You are worthy of none of them, but the rich and abundant grace of God was upon you, far above any merits of yours. Hail to you! Blessed are you, from henceforth and forever, in finding such a God.[6]

Nor was Luther alone. In Zurich the iconoclastic Zwingli (1484–1531) retained the *Hail Mary* in public worship. In some Lutheran orders the feast of the Immaculate Conception and the Assumption were retained well into the latter part of the sixteenth century. I need not here speak of the profound cult of Mary in the Greek and Russian churches and throughout the Middle East. All points to the consistency with which the *ecclesia orans* has honored the mother of God.

I believe that the notion of a Mary usurping the place of Jesus comes later than the Reformation and coincides with the loss of a truly mystical mentality in the West. The mania for dividing things in an either-or way is sometimes (rightly or wrongly) attributed to Descartes. "You can have this or that; but you cannot have both: Jesus *or* Mary but not Jesus *and* Mary." What a disastrous dualism! Whereas primitive and medieval Christianity could see *the mystery of Christ* as a single entity including many mysteries—the Trinity, the Incarnation, the Redemption, the mystery of Jesus, the mystery of Mary—post-Cartesian theological thought began to chop everything up. And so we find a split not only between Jesus and Mary but even between God and His creation.

I myself reacted against this either-or mentality when I came East and met Zen. As you probably know, Zen abhors the divisions of the discriminating intellect and stresses the unity of being. I believe that dialogue with Zen helps us regain that mystical sense of oneness whereby we have no difficulty in accepting both Jesus and Mary.

Let me add that from the earliest times Mary was invoked as ark of the covenant and tabernacle of the Most High. She is filled with the presence of God. She is filled with the Holy Spirit. In her womb dwells the Word made flesh. All these symbols point clearly to the union of Mary with the Trinity and especially with her Son who is the Word. The thought of a Mary separated from the Trinity and from Jesus was totally foreign to the early Christian mentality, as it is foreign to any mystical mentality.

## IV

Let me now describe how Marian devotion develops in the hearts of the faithful. These may begin with vocal prayer to Mary—reciting the rosary, or the litany of Loreto, or consecrating self to the Virgin Mary. And through this they may arrive at a certain intimacy with Mary whereby they speak spontaneously to her in times of trouble, asking for her help and protection. In an interview with *Time*, Lech Walesa, talking about his struggle with the authorities in Poland, speaks of his relationship with Mary. "When things got tragic or critical, I would say, 'Mother Mary, I'm losing, now what are you going to do about it?' Then I would take some time for myself. And I would say, 'What will be, will be. OK, it's your thing. How will you solve this?' "[7] Then he would relax with the reflection that there was a leader other than himself: the Virgin Mary. Such intimacy with Mary informs, as it has always informed, the lives of countless Christians.

As intimacy grows, words become less necessary and we may simply find ourselves in the presence of Mary—an all-pervading presence, a feminine presence, a warm and loving presence. Earlier in this book I spoke of the so-called acquired and infused contemplation. I said that a time comes when contemplation is not something I *do* but something that *happens*. Now, in the same way, the presence of Mary becomes a *given*. Not that I have a mental picture of what she looks like. I may have no image whatever. Like Gerard Manley Hopkins I may experience the presence of Mary like the air I breathe—"wild air, world-mothering air, nestling me everywhere." Turning to Mary I may cry out with the poet:

> Be thou then, O thou dear
> Mother, my atmosphere

Yes, Mary is now the atmosphere in which I walk—a feminine atmosphere, a protecting atmosphere, a guiding atmosphere, a loving atmosphere.

It may be that at this time one prays by contemplating a symbol of Mary. I have spoken already of a form of contemplation consisting of "presence to a symbol" and at that time I spoke of presence to the Eucharist. Now let me add that there is a prayer of "just being" in the presence of Mary, "just being" in the protective love of Mary. Presence to Mary. One may be present to a Marian ikon. Or one may hold the rosary in one's hand. The sense of Marian presence is an altered state of consciousness. With it we are at the gates of mysticism.

But can we authentically speak of a Marian mysticism?

Here let me be clear. Earlier in this book I have associated mysticism with the unconditional, unrestricted love that goes on and on and on. Clearly, such love can be directed to God and to God alone. Consequently we can never say that Mary is the object of mystical experience. What we can say, however, is that Mary is our mystical guide, our mystical traveling companion, our mystical protectress. She has been invoked as Our Lady of the Way. She can be compared to the cloud by day and the pillar of fire by night that guided the children of Israel through that great and terrible wilderness to the promised land. In short, Mary leads us beyond herself into the cloud of unknowing which is the mystery of her Son, as it is the mystery of the Father and the Holy Spirit. Entering this mystery and united with Jesus, we cry out: "Abba, Father!"

At this point, as we enter the night, Mary seems to disappear from consciousness. Of course she is present. But her presence is no longer tangible. We know that she is present not because we sense that all-pervasive closeness—"Be thou ... my atmosphere"—but because of dark faith.

Through Jesus to the Father, with Mary as mystical companion. It is a beautiful path and a secure path. But it is not a rose garden. It may even be full of conflict and temptation. But Mary is the health of the sick, the refuge of sinners, the comfort of the afflicted, the help of Christians. She is at once most powerful and most faithful. When she is present, all is well.

Yet I do not say that this Marian path is the way of all Christians. On the journey to God there are many charisms, many gifts. In the lives of some Christian mystics, Mary remains in the background, imperceptibly present, not tangibly so. In the lives of others, her presence manifests itself forcibly at one period in their lives and then falls into the background. But she is always there—becaues she shares preeminently in the mystery of Christ into which the Christian mystic is necessarily drawn.

But can we speak of a certain pattern in this Marian mystical experience?

## V

Earlier I tried to say that all Christian mystical experience is modelled on the covenant. God loves me with an everlasting love. His fidelity reaches to the skies and His love will never fail. I open my heart to accept this love and, having accepted it, I love Him in return—with that unconditional, unrestricted love that goes on and on and on. Through this love I enter into altered states of consciousness as I relish that all-embracing and enveloping presence. Presence leads to union. I become one with God. Yet I am not God.

Looking at Marian mysticism in the light of this model, we see that the first step consists not in loving Mary, but in accepting her love. As in all mysticism the initiative comes from God Who gives consolation without previous cause, so in this Marian path the initiative comes from Mary who enters our lives in a gratuitous way. As the wounded stag appears on the hill, so also on the hill appears one of whom it was said, "And a sword will pierce through your own soul also" (Luke 2:35). As Jesus was wounded with love, so Mary also is wounded with love for us.

The second step consists in loving her in return. While relishing her presence, fragrant like the air we breathe and warm as the atmosphere around us, we enter into altered states of consciousness whereby with her we recite our *Fiat*, with her we recite our *Magnificat*, with her we ponder in our hearts the mysteries of Jesus. With her we go through Jesus to the Father: "Abba, Father!" And in this way we undergo a profound metanoia and are transformed.

This love for Mary terminates at the Father. But it is authentic love for Mary, just as when we love people for God, we authentically love those people. Let me mention some characteristics of this Marian mystical love.

Traditionally love for Mary is associated with chastity. But chastity in the earliest tradition was not primarily centered on sexuality as it is today. The author of *The Cloud* calls a woman unchaste when she loves her husband for his money and not for himself. Chaste and perfect love, the great ideal of St. Bernard and the galaxy of mystics who surrounded him, was "disinterested love." It was the love of which Jesus spoke when he said: "If you loved me, you would have rejoiced, because I go to the Father" (John 14:28). Such love is totally centered on the beloved; yet paradoxically it brings true happiness and leads to the discovery of the true self.

Chastity or chaste love is mystical experience. St. Ignatius tells us that shortly after his conversion he had a mystical vision of Mary which brought a total liberation. Ignatius was slow to accept the authenticity of his own visions; but this one brought such remarkable fruits of liberation that he felt confident that it was the work of the Virgin herself. So powerful is the love of Mary for us and so powerful is the love she calls forth in our hearts.

Here let me pause to make a comment on chastity. It will be remembered that I said that love for poverty is a mystical experience, but that we obscured this mystical dimension with rules and regulations and guilt trips of all kinds. Similarly I said that love for peace is originally a mystical experience, but we obscured it with casuistic rules about just wars and the legitimacy of killing people in certain circumstances. Now let me say that chastity also was originally a mystical experience, an experience of mystical love. But we obscured it with all kinds of *do's* and *don'ts* about sexuality which obscured the mystical dimension of chaste love, and often caused anguishing scrupulosity and guilt to the most innocent people. Alas for legalism! Alas for pharisaism!

Chaste love is modelled on the love of Mary herself. While we poor human beings lost the image of God in which humanity was originally created, Mary never lost this God-like image. Her love was disinterested from the beginning. She was immaculate.

Again, love for Mary is love for the whole church of which

she is the model. It is not an exclusive Mary-and-I love, but a love stretching out to baptized Christians, to Jews, to Moslems, to Hindus, to Buddhists, and to all men and women of goodwill. The universal or social dimension of Marian love appears in the sayings of the great mystical visionaries of our times. These speak of Mary's concern for a world moving towards nuclear war and total destruction. The keynote of their message is that peace will only come through prayer and conversion of heart: "Pray! Pray! Pray!"

## VI

But let me speak about the doctrine of the Assumption, defined by Pius XII in the apostolic constitution *Munificentissimus Deus* in 1950. This constitution speaks of Mary as the new Eve who "although subject to the new Adam is most intimately associated with him in the struggle against the infernal foe." It goes on to say that just as the resurrection of Jesus was an essential part and the final sign of his victory, so it was fitting that "the struggle which was common to the Blessed Virgin and her divine Son should be brought to a close by the glorification of her virginal body."

As can be readily seen, the constitution associates Mary with the redemptive work of Jesus and claims that just as the body of Jesus rose, so the body of Mary was assumed into heaven. Karl Rahner explains the doctrine by calling Mary "the perfectly redeemed and the representative of perfect redemption." He writes that Mary "has entered into that perfect fulfillment which every Christian hopes for from the grace of God, as the outcome and fruit of human life."[8]

Remember that when Paul speaks of the resurrection of Jesus, he speaks in the same breath of the resurrection of the human family. "For if the dead are not raised, then Christ has not been raised" (1 Corinthians 15:16). As Jesus rose, we also will rise.

And the apostolic constitution tells us that Mary "even now" has achieved this state of glorification.

Now all this is important for understanding the sense of Marian presence about which I have spoken. Just as the Risen Jesus is present with us in his glorified body, just as he walks with us through life on our way to Emmaus, so Mary assumed into heaven is "even now" present with us in her glorified body. That is why we can compare her to the air we breathe. That is why we can believe that she guides us through life like the cloud by day and the pillar of fire by night. She is the perfectly redeemed.

Having said all this, however, let me confess that the doctrine of the Assumption has been the subject of controversy, a cruel bone of contention. Among its enthusiastic supporters, however, we find no less a person than Carl Jung who speaks of the 1950 definition as "the most important religious event since the Reformation."[9] Jung's theology is often unorthodox (how could it be otherwise?), but underlying the unorthodox theology are jewels of psychological and theological insight.

Jung was fascinated by the way in which the doctrine came to be defined. Pius XII claimed that he received petitions from the whole Catholic world begging for definition of a doctrine that had been in the hearts of the people for more than a millenium and that was part of their living faith. The Pope saw here the action of the Holy Spirit speaking through the masses of the people in union with their shepherds. Once again it was a question of the *sensus fidelium*, the *ecclesia orans*. Once again it was *vox populi: vox Dei*.

Now Jung saw this *sensus fidelium* as the collective unconscious of the church. It was perfectly obvious, he wrote, that for some time there has been a deep longing in the masses for the glorification of the feminine, a longing to recognize Mary as Queen of Heaven. "Anyone who has followed with attention

the visions of Mary which have been increasing in numbers over
the past few decades, and has taken their psychological significance into account, might have known what was brewing. The
fact especially that it was largely children who had the visions
might have given pause for thought, for in such cases the collective unconscious is always at work."[10] In defining the doctrine,
he claimed, the Catholic church was obviously listening to the
people.

As can be seen, the historical-critical approach, which was
later to hold the field in scriptural and patristic studies, played
a minimal part in the definition. This delighted Jung. "The
dogma of the Assumption is a slap in the face for the historical
and rationalistic view of the world, and would remain so for all
time if one were to insist obstinately on the arguments of reason
and history."[11]

He goes on to say that in accepting living tradition as a theological source and in remaining in touch with the movements of
the Holy Spirit, Catholicism manifests her maternal spirit,
whereas the Protestant emphasis on reason manifests a paternal
spirit. And he concludes with an ecumenical and almost humor-
ous plea for union and cooperation between sister and brother.

Let me add, however, that Jung wrote in the 1950s and that
the tables have turned since then. Now Catholic scholars immersed in the historical-critical approach are in danger of losing
their sense of archetype and symbol, whereas Protestant scholars
move towards the sense of mystery. Perhaps Jung's brother-and-
sister prophecy is becoming a reality.

## VII

Since Jung wrote confidently about the unconscious
longing in the masses for the exaltation of the Mother of God,
psychologists and theologians everywhere have come to recognize the importance of the feminine dimension in religious

experience. Just as in our affective lives we need masculine and feminine influence in order to grow, so in our religious lives we need this dual influence. Chinese philosophy reminds us of this. It insists that there must be balance between the *yin* and the *yang* in the human body, in the human psyche, in culture, in politics, in economics—and, we might add, in the approach to God. Without this balance, men and women can become sick. Without this balance, the whole culture can become sick.

Now the fact is that Christian symbols, as we now use them, are largely masculine. Realizing that this could cause imbalance, psychologists and theologians are studying the feminine in God. They speak of God not only as father but also as mother. They see the Holy Spirit, *Sophia*, as a feminine principle. These studies are only beginning. I believe they are of crucial importance for the future of theology and for the future of world culture.

And yet the feminine dimension in God is not enough. We need a feminine dimension in redemption. If our prayer is to be fully human we need not only a man of flesh and blood who was like us in all things except sin—who was weary, tempted, and rejected; we also need a woman of flesh and blood to whom we can turn in time of need. Traditionally this woman has been Mary. She has been "our life, our sweetness and our hope." She has been the health of the sick, the refuge of sinners, the comfort of the afflicted, the help of Christians.

And in all this she plays a role that Jesus cannot play. This may sound offensive to pious ears which rightly stress the unique mediatorship of Jesus. But I ask you to reflect that, in becoming flesh, the Word took on the limitations of flesh. He was a Jew, born in a certain country, speaking a certain language, educated in a certain culture, and thinking according to certain cultural patterns. And included in these limitations is the fact that he was a man, not a woman. And so the Catholic tradition has held that he entrusted the feminine role to Mary, not because she was equal to him as mediator, but because he loved her and he loves us.

And so the masses of the people have always prayed to Mary. If one goes to the great shrines of Mary throughout the world; if one goes to Guadalupe or Lourdes or Fatima; if one goes to Quiapo or Baclaran here in Manila; if one watches the prayer of the people, it is difficult to deny that the Holy Spirit is present and that Mary is present. She is indeed our life, our sweetness, and our hope.

## NOTES

1. *Lumen Gentium* C.8, 56; *The Documents of Vatican II*, ed. Walter M. Abbot (New York: America Press, 1966), p. 88.
2. Ibid; ibid., p. 90.
3. Ibid; ibid., p. 92.
4. Ibid.; ibid., p. 87.
5. John J. Elliott, "The Image of Mary: A Lutheran View," *America*, New York, March 27, 1982.
6. Ibid.
7. "An Interview with Lech Walesa," *Time*, New York, January 4, 1982.
8. See Karl Rahner, *Theological Investigations: Vol. I God, Christ, Mary, and Grace* (New York: Seabury; London: Darton, Longman and Todd, 1961), p. 224 ff.
9. C. G. Jung, *Answer to Job* (Princeton: Princeton Univ. Press, 1969), p. 464.
10. Ibid., p. 461.
11. Ibid., p. 467.

# Epilogue

The stag appears on the hill, wounded and thirsty and longing for cool waters. He is wounded with compassion; he is wounded with love.

Jesus is the wounded stag. And Christian mysticism begins and ends with the mystery of his cross and the mystery of his great love. This is the love which reveals the Father. This is the love which impels him to lay down his life for his friends. This is the love from which neither death, or life, nor angels, nor principalities, nor things present, nor things to come can separate us.

And the love of God in Christ Jesus creates something new in us. It makes us cry out in ecstasy: "Jesus is Lord!" It makes us identify with Jesus in the intimate call: "Abba, Father!" It effects a change of heart and a revolution in consciousness whereby we are totally and radically and foolishly committed to the gospel. In the modern world it effects a change of heart and a revolution in consciousness whereby we are totally and radically committed to peace. As today there is no living Christianity without a living commitment to peace, so there is no mystical Christianity without a mystical commitment to peace.

In this book I have written about the social implications of Christian mysticism. In particular I have written about poverty and peace, illustrating my point with a chapter on the anguishing conflict in Ireland. If my reader is surprised that I write about Ireland, let him or her reflect that during my thirty years in Asia, the cruel suffering of my people in Ulster has never been far from my consciousness. I have been constantly aware of the love and the hate, the light and the darkness, the heroism and the degradation, the shining good and black evil which are alive in that heartrending conflict.

And yet the chapter on Ireland is more than an outlet for my pent-up feelings. I believe it has a message for everyone. I argue that the only answer to the agony of Ulster is a total and radical commitment to the gospel on the part of a significant number of people on both sides of the border and on both sides of the Irish Sea. I thought this said everything until a New York friend who read my manuscript commented that conversion of heart on both sides of the border and on both sides of the Irish Sea is not sufficient. We need conversion, he said, on both sides of the Atlantic.

And then I realized anew that the problems of Ireland are the problems of the world. Everywhere we need conversion. Everywhere we need total commitment to peace. It is a question of survival. And this total conversion and radical commitment will not come from an enlightened assessment of the military potential of the superpowers. It will not come from studying the just war theories of the old moralists. It will not come from wild panic at the awful consequences of nuclear conflagration. All this might help. But the crucial thing is a radical, foolish, and mystical love for the gospel.

I concluded this book with a chapter on one whose eyes are fixed on the wounded stag. She asks for a radical commitment to the gospel when she says quite simply: "Do whatever he tells you" (John 2:5). With these words she describes the path of Christian mysticism and shows us the way to peace.

# Index

# Acknowledgments

Many people helped me with this book. I wish especially to express my gratitude to Tom O'Gorman, Frank Sammon, Lin Huei–Mei, and John Brannigan who read my manuscript making helpful suggestions for improvement, to Candy de la Cruz, who drew the maps and sketch which appear in the text, and to my community of Jesuit tertians who gave me constant encouragement while I was writing. Let me above all express my gratitude to the people of the Philippines who have welcomed me to their country. Their deep religious faith and their unfailing hospitality have let me see that Christianity has entered deeply into the hearts of an Asian people and will bring forth much fruit in a new world which is painfully coming to birth.

*Manila*
*March 25, 1983*